Photojournalism

LIFE LIBRARY OF PHOTOGRAPHY

Photojournalism

BY THE EDITORS OF TIME-LIFE BOOKS

TIME-LIFE BOOKS, NEW YORK

ON THE COVER: A routine political rally and a sensational tragedy are both reported in this contact sheet from one roll of film taken by LIFE photographer Bill Eppridge. It shows Senator Robert F. Kennedy speaking in Los Angeles on June 5, 1968, and then lying in a corridor after being shot. From these scenes came a classic of photojournalism, frame 27 *(outlined in color),* reproduced in enlarged form on page 30.

Contents

Portions of this book were written by William
Cahn and Leonard McCombe. Valuable aid was
provided by these individuals and departments
of Time Inc.: Editorial Production, Norman
Airey, Margaret T. Fischer; Library, Peter Draz;
Picture Collection, Doris O'Neil; Photo
Equipment Supervisor, Albert Schneider; TIME-
LIFE News Service, Murray J. Gart;
Correspondents Elisabeth Kraemer (Bonn),
Maria Vincenza Aloisi (Paris), Margot Hapgood
(London), Ann Natanson (Rome),
Jean Bratten (Madrid), Friso Endt (Amsterdam),
James Wilde (Nairobi).

As this book was going to press, one of its editors chanced to take a walk with one of the world's great photojournalists, Alfred Eisenstaedt. The two men tramped for a number of miles through woods and along the seashore, Eisenstaedt lugging a heavy bag that held two cameras and numerous lenses, the editor empty-handed. As it happened, the light that day was not interesting and Eisenstaedt did not take a single picture. However, he was ready, as he always is. He has carried a camera constantly for 40 years and for hundreds of thousands of miles, and has taken numberless memorable pictures, many of which he had no idea he would get when he started out. The editor—who seldom carries a camera except when he decides "to go out and take pictures"—has a slender file of memorable shots but a very large collection of missed opportunities.

Many amateurs have the technical skills and the imagination of professionals, and certainly all the equipment they need. But they don't take as good pictures. This stems largely from a difference in attitude. The professional must sell his pictures. Therefore he constantly thinks about them. If he is a photojournalist he develops the ability to regard them not so much as individual pictures but as parts of larger subjects, and he is always considering how and where they may be published.

It is this difference in attitude that ultimately distinguishes the professional. It forces him to stand outside himself, to think like an editor, to ask himself if what he has framed in his viewfinder is really a "useful" picture, if it helps tell a story, establish a mood, catch the high point of an event. In short, the effort to think like a professional teaches him how to squeeze the maximum out of what is going on around him. That is what photojournalism is—making photographic stories out of events and their impact on people.

Its disciplines can improve the work of any photographer, for while they are sometimes hard to practice, they are not hard to learn and they are simple in outline. First, do what Alfred Eisenstaedt does: carry a camera. Second, go where the action is. The great news pictures in the first chapter of this book were taken by people who, one way or another, had made it their business to be where things were happening. The happening may be only a sunset, but if it catches the photographer empty-handed it will go unrecorded. Third, try to turn single pictures into multipicture stories and to anticipate events in order to build up such stories. Fourth, be critical of the results, applying the standards of the editor or advertising man who buys pictures. If the pictures are below par or just plain dull, put them aside. Be ruthless in selection, particularly when making up slide shows of color transparencies (but don't ignore the discards; they provide valuable lessons about how to work more effectively). The photographer who does these things will be practicing photojournalism, whether he realizes it or not. And almost certainly that practice will make him a better photographer.

The Editors

PHOTOGRAPHER UNKNOWN: *Photographers covering Ohio River flood,* 1937

Reporter with a Camera

We take photographic reporting for granted today. When a war breaks out, men land on the moon, a king is crowned or a football championship won, we expect to see pictures of the event in the next newspaper or magazine that we buy. And spot news is only one of many courses on our accustomed pictorial menu. The fare may include reportage on anything from the alluring looks of a new actress to the migration habits of polar bears, from slum conditions in New York to religious rites in Mecca. Our appetite for the fruits of photojournalism is so great that reportorial pictures appear on book jackets, calendars, postcards and advertisements—in short, virtually everywhere that ink meets paper.

Photojournalism shows us things that we would not ordinarily see; it takes us to places where we would not normally go; it explains the enormously complicated warp and woof of the world. No locale is too distant, no conditions are too arduous to deter the photojournalist. Sometimes, of course, his dauntless curiosity gets him in trouble. Francis Miller of the Houston *Press* got his comeuppance some years ago when he was covering a trial in a Houston courtroom where cameras were not permitted. He had, in past adventures, secreted his miniature camera in a flamboyant necktie, an elegant cigarette case or a hollowed-out novel. Unfortunately, a member of the underworld who was familiar with these exploits happened to be at the trial, and he cried out, "Hey, Miller, where you got the camera hid this time?" No pictures were to be had that day.

That anyone would even want a picture of a sensational trial is a relatively new idea. News and pictures were not always regarded as natural partners. The beginnings of photojournalism can be seen in the drawings and cartoons that occasionally appeared in the drab 18th Century press. Benjamin Franklin, when he was publishing the *Pennsylvania Gazette* in the 1750s, printed a woodcut of a snake chopped into many pieces over the caption, "Join, or die." That was scarcely spot news, but it at least touched one of the major concerns of the time: the necessity of unity in the American colonies. In 1770 after the Boston Massacre, Paul Revere, who was not only a patriot and silversmith but an able engraver, produced a dramatic plate showing British troops firing on a crowd of civilians. The engraving would have made a dandy news picture—if it had only been printed in a newspaper. But Revere did not see fit to give it to the *Boston Gazette*. He merely sold individual copies of it for eight pence apiece, and gave the *Gazette* a small, dull picture of five coffins, memorializing the citizens killed in the massacre.

What is very likely the first specimen of the modern news picture appeared in *The Illustrated London News* in 1842, the year of its founding *(opposite)*. Prophetically, in view of the nature of so many of the news pictures that have followed it, it showed an act of violence—a would-be assassin firing a pistol

The first spot news picture ever to appear in a newspaper was a drawing in The Illustrated London News of an assassination attempt on Queen Victoria on May 30, 1842. The Queen and her consort, Prince Albert, were riding in their carriage in London when a young man suddenly drew a pistol from his waistcoat and leveled it at them. An alert constable saved the Queen's life by knocking the weapon from the man's hand.

at Queen Victoria. Although daguerreotypes had then been known for a few years, there was no camera that could possibly have caught the action. The picture was simply an artist's version of what had happened.

The Illustrated London News picture was not hailed by everyone as a triumph. Soon William Wordsworth, Poet Laureate of England, took to grumbling about pictures in the press. Wordsworth thought illustrations of that sort were in exceedingly poor taste and that people who were fed a diet of pictures might forget the important things, reading and writing. He said so in a sonnet called "Illustrated Books and Newspapers," which goes, in part:

> Now prose and verse sunk into disrepute
> Must lackey a dumb Art that best can suit
> The taste of this once-intellectual Land.
> A backward movement surely have we here,
> From manhood, —back to childhood . . .
> Avaunt this vile abuse of pictured page!
> Must eyes be all in all, the tongue and ear
> Nothing? Heaven keep us from a lower stage!

Wordsworth's reaction was soon echoed across the Channel. When a famous French tragedienne known simply as Rachel died on January 4, 1858, a photographer sneaked into her bedroom and took a picture of the corpse. An artist's rendition of the picture appeared in a newspaper a few days later —and the family of the actress were so outraged that they brought suit and won damages for "invasion of privacy."

In addition to a lack of enthusiasm in certain quarters, picture journalism faced other obstacles, among them the problem of how to get the picture onto the printed page. Woodcuts were the standard means of reproduction, both in England and the United States, where *Frank Leslie's Illustrated Newspaper* and *Harper's Weekly* got into the business in the 1850s. Although woodcutting would seem to have little to do with photography, the two were associated for many years, and it is well to have a look at the process.

At first photography was not involved at all. In reporting a news event, an artist would go to the scene and make a rough sketch. From this he would make a finished drawing suitable for woodcutting, in which straight, heavy lines were emphasized and shadows were indicated by many small, separate strokes. Next he would copy the drawing, sometimes in reverse, on a smooth block, usually of boxwood, and a skilled craftsman would then cut away all of the surface except the lines that were to be printed. The finished block was pressed into soft clay, and a cast was made by pouring molten type metal onto the fresh impression. This cast—or stereotype—could be put on a newspaper or magazine press and would make thousands of copies.

When the camera came into widespread use in the 1840s, photographs did not revolutionize picture journalism—far from it. The engraving and printing processes of the time could not reproduce a photograph on ordinary paper, alongside ordinary type, on an ordinary press. Only the full tones of the photograph, the solid blacks and blank whites could be rendered. The intermediate shades of gray—called halftones—could not. Consequently, photographs had to be converted into drawings and then into woodcuts before they could appear as news pictures *(right and opposite)*. The photograph merely furnished material for the artist, taking the place of the on-the-scene sketch the artist had formerly made.

Advances in technology were required before photojournalism could become a major force, and the necessary inventions did not come into widespread use until the turn of the century. Meanwhile, since illustrations in the press were still held in Wordsworthian contempt by many, the popular taste for them had to be cultivated. The cultivation was done in large part by one man, Joseph Pulitzer, who in 1883 bought the money-losing New York *World* and within three years turned it into the most profitable paper ever published. Although he is revered today for his endowment of the Columbia School of Journalism and the Pulitzer Prizes, he was also the grandfather of all sensationalists. He splattered his pages with stories of blood and crime, for which he invented the X-marks-the-spot diagram: "A) Door stained with blood B) Window stained with blood C) Bed covered with blood D) Table set and covered with blood. . . ." Pulitzer also regaled his readers with pictures of criminals or suspects—very accurate pictures, it turned out. In 1884 a detective in Montreal arrested a New York stockbroker who had fled to Canada after indictment for fraud, recognizing him from a *World* woodcut. In the same year Ontario police, using another *World* picture, put the arm on a notorious fugitive fence named "Marm" Mandelbaum. Rejoicing, Pulitzer said, "Thus, while we are contributing our share toward the advancement of American art and are educating as well as amusing our numerous readers, we are subserving the cause of public justice. . . ."

Pulitzer recognized, too, that pictures of noncriminals may be of legitimate news interest, and began to print portraits of ministers, teachers, lawyers, actors and political figures. But when he went so far as to display a gallery of pretty girls from the neighboring city of Brooklyn, "Ladies Who Grace and Adorn the Social Circle," he ran into trouble. *The Journalist,* a trade paper that worried about the morals of the press, felt "The *World* made an error of no small magnitude when it published its series of Brooklyn Belles. . . . On Monday morning after the objectionable pictures appeared, the studio of the photographer who made the pictures from which the draw-

When this photographic portrait of Abraham Lincoln was made by Mathew Brady in 1860, the picture could be reproduced on the printed page only by first converting it into a woodcut, as Harper's Weekly did for the cover of its November 10 issue (right). The woodcut contained every detail of Lincoln's pose, but the engraver exercised artistic license on the rest of the picture. He supplied a new background, with draperies and a scenic view, and he did not compensate for the reversal that occurs in printing, causing the reproduction to become a mirror image of the original photograph.

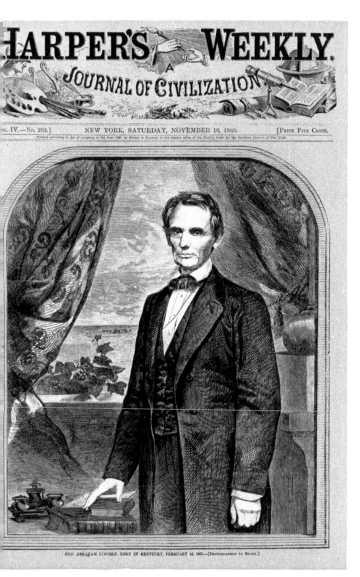

ings were obtained, was thronged by an anxious and angry crowd of fathers, brothers, husbands and lovers, all breathing dire vengeance upon the photographer. . . .

"It is a piece of glaring bad taste for a newspaper to invade the sanctity of the home circle and hold up to public gaze and mayhap ridicule the portraits of young ladies who in no wise court publicity, and in whom the public has no interest except as they are pretty women. . . .

"It is just this sort of journalism that fosters the idea in the minds of the general public that a newspaper man has no conscience, and that when he enters the house it is a good time to lock up the spoons."

The photographer evidently escaped from the affair with his life—there is no record that he was even horsewhipped—and Pulitzer went right on printing pictures of ladies who adorn the social circle. What he had noticed was that, as he put it, "in the midst of all the newspaper interviewing, editorial twaddling and legal flapdoodling touching the artistic presentation . . . we have received no complaints from the charming and worthy ladies whose portraits graced our pages."

Pulitzer's *World* soon became so heavily illustrated that pictures were among its most important elements—pictures of sidewalk peddlers, trained dogs, German bands and President Chester A. Arthur's wardrobe exclusive of his underwear. The *World* even got hold of Arthur's hand-written notes for one of his speeches and printed them in facsimile, explaining that this was done so that readers "may become familiar with the chirography of the President of the United States."

As Pulitzer warmed up the audience, technology weighed in with a number of innovations that really got photojournalism moving. In the closing years of the 19th Century there came into common use better portable cameras and easier-to-handle plates, as well as roll film. *Blitzlichtpulver*—a mixture of magnesium powder, potassium chlorate and antimony sulfide that gave a brilliant flash of light when ignited—was invented in Germany and was soon being used to make pictures at night or in dim interiors. But what mattered most was the perfection of a means of reproducing photographs on the printed page directly, without having to enlist an artist to convert them into woodcuts. Inventors had been working on such a technique for years. Their aim was to find some way of reproducing on newsprint the grays—or halftones—of photographic images. The solution (illustrated on the following pages) was to use a ruled glass screen to break up the image into myriads of dots, some tiny, some large. On January 21, 1897, the New York *Tribune* published the first halftone reproduction to appear in a mass circulation daily paper; it was a rather dull photograph of Thomas C. Platt, a New Yorker who had just been elected to the United States Senate. Ten days later, the paper deepened its commitment to the new process by publishing pictures of grim, dirty tenements that housed many of the city's poor. For the first time, a mass audience was seeing pictures that carried the convincing sense of realism unique to photography; no artist or engraver was acting as a middleman between the readers and the facts recorded by the camera.

It might be expected that the halftone process would sweep through journalism; it did not. Publishers thought their readers would consider the halftone a cheap substitute for hand art. Also, newspapers had a substantial investment in the artists and engravers who had drawn news pictures: in 1891 there were 1,000 artists turning out more than 10,000 drawings a week for the press. They continued to copy photographs for several years after the halftone had been proved practical. When the battleship *Maine* was blown up in Havana harbor in 1898, Pulitzer's *World* was on the streets five days after the incident with "the first actual photographs of the wreck"—which were in fact carefully drawn simulations of photographs. A week passed before the papers offered halftones made from the photographs themselves.

But after a few years of hesitation, the press embraced halftones with all its heart, and by 1910 the old hand engraving was headed for oblivion. Actual views of the great events of the day became regular front-page fare. When the *Titanic* sank in 1912, the papers were filled with halftones showing the passengers who had been aboard and the rescue efforts that took place in the freezing north Atlantic. When American troops were sent to Europe in 1917, photographers were on hand to record their arrival. The Sunday rotogravure section of *The New York Times,* in particular, devoted much of its space to photographic coverage of World War I developments. When President Woodrow Wilson signed the Treaty of Versailles in 1918, two other New York papers joined together in a bold attempt to beat their competitors with pictures of the event. The photographs were carried to New York by the first blimp ever to cross the Atlantic.

Photojournalists also began to probe into the darker side of society. No one stirred the American conscience more effectively than freelance photographer Lewis W. Hine. A series of his pictures, appearing in a magazine called *Charities and the Commons* in 1908, showed how millions of immigrants had to live in overcrowded slums and eke out pitiful wages at enslaving jobs. While Lewis Hine and other muckraking photojournalists peered at the depths of America, other photojournalists began to venture far afield. The *National Geographic,* a rather stodgy journal that came out at unpredictable intervals at the turn of the century, ran its first halftone in 1903 —a picture of Philippine women working in a rice field. The response was so favorable that the magazine soon had swarms of photographers circling the globe to bring back for stay-at-homes pictures of exotic lands and cultures.

How the halftone process converts the continuous shades of gray in a photograph into distinct units of black and white that can be printed with ink on paper is illustrated in these details of a picture of actress Sophia Loren. First, the original (above, left) is rephotographed through a "screen"—a plate of clear plastic crosscut with a grid pattern. The grid, by optical principles still not fully understood, breaks the continuous tones of the picture into dots (above, right). This scheme of dots is then transferred chemically onto a printing plate.

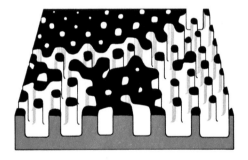

This detail of the printing plate, which shows the portion of the picture outlined at top right, indicates how the chemicals have etched a pattern that conforms to the dot scheme. Only the dots transfer ink to the paper in most printing processes. Since the dots are larger and thus their edges closer together in areas that were dark in the original, those areas transfer more ink to the paper—and print darker —than other sections, approximating the shading in the original photograph.

This picture has purposely been made with a very coarse screen so that the dot structure of the image can easily be seen. Greater fidelity to the original can be obtained by using a more closely ruled screen, thus increasing the number of dots in the picture. Ordinarily, black-and-white reproductions in the LIFE Library of Photography are made with a 150-line screen (one ruled with a grid of 150 lines per inch); the dots in them can be detected only with a magnifying glass, making the pictures virtually indistinguishable from the originals.

But serious edification of the public was not the only concern of the growing corps of photojournalists. The lessons learned by Joseph Pulitzer were put to good use. The year 1919 saw the appearance in New York of a paper with a word-and-picture tabloid format, the *Illustrated Daily News* (later called the *Daily News*). The front page of the first issue offered a huge picture of the Prince of Wales announcing his forthcoming visit to Newport. The back page was entirely devoted to pictures of beauty-contest entrants. Subsequent issues more than lived up to this zesty overture, and by 1924 the *Daily News* had the largest circulation of any United States newspaper, titillating an eager public with well-illustrated stories on marital problems, crime news and sex. But for sheer sensationalism, it paled beside another tabloid of the 20s, the New York *Evening Graphic,* which carried the themes of sex and violence about as far as they could go (readers nicknamed it the Pornographic). The *Graphic's* main contribution to photojournalistic history was the composograph—a fake picture made by pasting several photographs together. One of the most famous composographs, inspired by the attempt of a wealthy manufacturer, Edward West "Daddy" Browning, to leave his 15-year-old wife "Peaches" on the ground that Peaches had insisted her mother live with them, showed the couple cavorting in a bedroom, with mother eavesdropping outside the door.

In their sensationalistic heyday, the tabloids would do just about anything to get a genuine shocker of a photograph. A case in point is the New York *Daily News* photograph of Ruth Snyder dying in the electric chair. Mrs. Snyder, who was convicted of murdering her husband in a thunderously publicized "love-triangle" trial, was sentenced to be electrocuted in Sing Sing Prison, New York. Although pictures of people being executed were prohibited—not by law, but by custom and the warden's directive—the management of the *News* decided to photograph the event.

Getting a man on the scene was not difficult. Pencil reporters are invited to executions; camera reporters, however, are not. Consequently the *News* photographer had to smuggle his camera into the electrocution room. Because the faces of *News* photographers were well known to the police, the editors decided to fetch an outsider, Tom Howard of the *Chicago Tribune,* to do the job. Howard was brought to New York a month ahead of time and installed in a hotel room, where he whiled away his time practicing sneak shots with a miniature camera. The camera, which was not loaded with film but with one glass plate smaller than a matchbook, was taped just above Howard's left ankle; thence a cable release ran up his trouser leg into his pocket. Howard aimed the camera by pointing his foot.

In addition to importing Howard and rigging the camera, the editors of the *News* somehow got hold of blueprints of the electrocution room—it was necessary to pre-focus the camera, and therefore some idea of Howard's position in relation to the chair was needed. On the night of the execution Howard walked into the room, well-nigh as familiar with it as with his own parlor, and took his predetermined place. When Mrs. Snyder was killed by temporarily being incorporated into a 2,200-volt circuit, Howard lifted his trouser leg and exposed the plate. If the picture *(right)* seems a trifle blurry, it is not because Howard flinched; not at all. It is because he coolly exposed the plate three times, for a total of about five seconds, to catch Mrs. Snyder's attitude as the current was applied, cut off and reapplied.

The questionable art of sneak photography has been carried on in modern times by a breed of Italian photojournalists known as *paparazzi,* who specialize in catching jet-setters off-guard. They got their name from Federico Fellini's classic film, *La Dolce Vita.* One of the minor characters in the film is an irksome photographer named Paparazzo who dashes about taking pictures of people in embarrassing situations. Fellini selected the name Paparazzo because, he explained, "It suggested a buzzing, stinging, annoying sort of insect, which was the idea I wanted to put across." An Italian word with a similar sound, *pappataci,* in fact means *gnat.*

Often, the buzz of the real *paparazzo* cannot be heard until it is too late. French siren Brigitte Bardot found this the case when she saw pictures of herself in the nude splashed across the pages of the Italian magazine *Playmen;* an enterprising *paparazzo* had tracked her to a holiday villa outside Rome and caught comely views from 600 feet away with a 640mm telephoto lens. Another target of the *paparazzi,* Elizabeth Taylor, hired detectives to protect her from them, but one determined snoop lowered himself by rope onto her hotel terrace to get pictures of the actress dining with her fourth husband, Eddie Fisher.

The *paparazzi* show equal skill at operating in the open. Racing on motorscooters from airport to restaurant to nightclub, they run down their famous prey with all the subtlety of a baying wolf pack. When the actor Ernest Borgnine quarreled with his wife on the streets of Rome, sufficient *paparazzi* were on hand to turn night into day with their popping flashbulbs. And should action not offer itself to their ubiquitous cameras, the *paparazzi* manufacture it. A favorite technique is to surround a celebrity, set off flashbulbs in his face and otherwise harass him until he actually hits one of his tormentors, and then document the provoked assault for the next day's front page. The method is painful, but usually lucrative. Italian magazines and newspapers pay as little as $5 for a straightforward portrait of a famous person—but a picture of a celebrity on the rampage brings as much as $500.

Working in the sensationalistic tradition of Pulitzer's *World,* the New York *Graphic* and other tabloids, the *paparazzi* raise anew the question of the

DAILY NEWS EXTRA
Sunday, 1,357,556
Daily, 1,193,297
Vol. 9. No. 173 36 Pages   New York, Friday, January 13, 1928   2 Cents

DEAD!

RUTH SNYDER'S DEATH PICTURED!—This is perhaps the most remarkable exclusive picture in the history of criminology. It shows the actual scene in the Sing Sing death house as the lethal current surged through Ruth Snyder's body at 11:06 last night. Her helmeted head is stiffened in death, her face masked and an electrode strapped to her bare right leg. The autopsy table on which her body was removed is beside her. Judd Gray, mumbling a prayer, followed her down the narrow corridor at 11:14. "Father, forgive them, for they don't know what they are doing?" were Ruth's last words. The picture is the first Sing Sing execution picture and the first of a woman's electrocution.

One of the most sensational news photographs ever published—and one of the first made with a concealed camera—is the picture of the electrocution of murderess Ruth Snyder that the New York Daily News spread across its front page on Friday, the 13th of January, 1928 (left). The close view reproduced by the News was greatly enlarged from a portion of a small negative, which is printed in its entirety above. Most of the negative shows only the legs of witnesses because the secret camera was strapped to the ankle of the photographer—but the close-up gives a vivid view of Mrs. Snyder.

proper limits of photojournalism. It is not an easy question. News photography has never found a final answer to the conflict between two fundamental rights: the right of the individual to privacy, and the right of the public to be informed. As far back as 1890 Samuel D. Warren and Louis D. Brandeis, later a Justice of the Supreme Court, noted in the *Harvard Law Review* that it had become possible "to take pictures surreptitiously." The technology of photography and printing had become so advanced that "instantaneous photographs and newspaper enterprise have invaded the sacred precincts of private and domestic life; and numerous mechanical devices threaten to make good the prediction that 'what is whispered in the closet shall be proclaimed from the housetops!' "

The article was wonderfully prescient. The authors had never heard the word *paparazzo,* and the most surreptitious photograph that could have been taken in a closet in 1890 would have been accompanied by a blast of *Blitzlichtpulver* sufficient to burn off a man's beard. Yet Brandeis and Warren could see, across the years, that some sort of reasonable limit had to be placed on the news camera.

Today it is generally held that public figures—politicians, actors and other celebrities who thrust themselves into the public eye—are fair game for photojournalists at virtually all times. They cannot have it both ways, cannot plead for publicity in the morning and expect not to be photographed in some embarrassing circumstance later in the day. There are many others who cannot claim total privacy from the news media—criminals, people accused of crime and people involved in accidents or disasters. However sad it may be, such individuals, in the words of one judge, "are subject to the privileges which publishers have to satisfy the curiosity of the public as to their leaders, heroes, villains and victims."

"The curiosity of the public" really refers to the right of the public to be informed. Who can say that a picture of the gory aftermath of tragedy may not contribute to the making of a law or agreement that will prevent another? But in this sort of situation, there are limits to informing the public. While a photographer can legitimately take pictures at the scene of an accident, he may be violating the right of privacy if he tries to pursue the victim into the ambulance or the emergency room. The ordinary uninjured, nonpublic figure is assumed to have, as a Kentucky judge has pointed out, "the right to be free from unwarranted publicity, or the right to live without unwarranted interference by the public about matters with which the public is not necessarily concerned." Such cautions are unlikely to change the photojournalist from what he usually is—a hardworking, brave and thoughtful fellow who is really working for *you.* If you should happen to see one, why, tip your hat to him. Please don't tip it in such a way that it hides your face; just tip it. □

News Photography—The Critical Moment

Great news photos distill the confused brew of human affairs. They extract from a war the one moment that speaks for all the horrors of all the battles; they snatch from a long political campaign the instant when a candidate most clearly reveals his character; they witness the extraordinary events—catastrophes, victories, pioneering expeditions—that determine the flavor of an entire era. Yet the photojournalist is not a historian who, from a detached vantage point, discerns the great currents of an age. Instead, he swims in the roiling sea of events along with his subjects—and often obtains his insights through quick reflexes or sheer luck.

As shown by the portfolio on the following pages, the subject matter of photojournalism is as varied as human experience itself. The critical moment caught by a photojournalist may be the detonation of an atomic bomb *(right),* the tears wept at a great man's funeral or the thrust of an assassin's sword. But all these news photos share one trait: they catch the essence of a person or event, and thereby leave an indelible mark on the mind of the viewer.

No news photographer, but an automatic camera, photographed a postwar atomic test near the Bikini Atoll in 1946 and gave the public a clear view of the fearsome destructive power of fission bombs. The underwater explosion lifted a solid column of water 5,500 feet above a fleet of junked warships placed in the target area. Bulkheads burst and superstructures were carried away as the ocean erupted— and seconds later 10 of the vessels sank.

Automatic Camera Recording of the Atomic Test at Bikini, 1946

Twentieth Century Milestones

JOHN D. DANIELS: *The First Airplane Flies*, 1903

Man's dream of powered flight came true on December 17, 1903, when Orville Wright flew a gawky contraption for 12 seconds at Kitty Hawk, North Carolina. Coast Guardsman John D. Daniels, from a nearby station, took the picture above just at the moment when brother Wilbur released the wing and the air age was born.

Sixty-six years after the Wrights' airplane wobbled aloft, astronaut Edwin E. (Buzz) Aldrin Jr. stood on the surface of the moon, 239,000 miles from home. Reflected in his visor (right) are pieces of scientific equipment, the moon-landing craft Eagle, and his fellow voyager Neil Armstrong, who took this photograph with a specially designed Hasselblad camera.

NEIL ARMSTRONG: *Buzz Aldrin on the Moon*, 1969

Surprising Triumphs in Politics

AL MUTO: *Truman Defeats Dewey*, 1948

The polls had predicted that Harry S Truman would lose to Thomas E. Dewey in the 1948 Presidential election—and the Chicago Daily Tribune went so far as to headline his defeat while votes were still being counted. Heading back to Washington after his victory, Truman showed the headline to cheering supporters in St. Louis with the obvious relish of a man who has had the last laugh—and was snapped in mid-laugh by Al Muto of International News Photos.

Wendell Willkie savored an unexpected—and brief—moment of glory in 1940 as he rode a motorcade through his home town of Elwood, Indiana, on the way to accept the Republican nomination for the Presidency. His supporters had won over the convention delegates by chanting "We want Willkie" so persistently that the hammerlock on the nomination held by Senator Robert A. Taft was broken, and political newcomer Willkie was selected to challenge the incumbent, Franklin D. Roosevelt.

JOHN D. COLLINS: *Wendell Willkie Motorcade, 1940*

A Step toward War

With military smartness, spade-carrying troops of the Labor Service march at the Nazi Party's 1937 congress in Nuremberg, as Adolf Hitler salutes from his Mercedes-Benz. The 500,000 members of the Labor Service had the job of building roads, clearing land and draining swamps in the resurgent Fatherland—but most of them were destined for service with the Wehrmacht. At the moment that a Nazi party photographer made this picture, Hitler was making plans for the invasion of Czechoslovakia.

PHOTOGRAPHER UNKNOWN: *Nazis on Parade*, 1937

All swagger and bluster, Italian dictator Benito
Mussolini addresses a crowd in 1938, wearing
the uniform of the Fascist militia that he
founded. The pose betrayed the bravado of
Mussolini, who had dodged the draft before
World War I and later, when he joined the army,
rose to the unexalted rank of corporal.

PHOTOGRAPHER UNKNOWN: *Benito Mussolini,* 1938

Simplicity and great moral force were the essential traits of Mohandas Gandhi, shown reading in his home at the age of 76 in this classic picture by Margaret Bourke-White of LIFE. Although he was the leader of India's long struggle to win independence from Britain, Gandhi spent one hour every afternoon working at the spinning wheel in the foreground.

MARGARET BOURKE-WHITE: *Gandhi*, 1946

Cigarette holder cocked jauntily above a half-smile, President Franklin D. Roosevelt is a vision of confidence at a Democratic fund-raising dinner in 1938. Although the United States was mired in a recession at the time, Roosevelt characteristically took the offensive in his speech at the dinner, inveighing against the selfish "handful" of big businessmen who wanted to run the country for their own good.

TOM McAVOY: *Franklin D. Roosevelt*, 1938

The Nightmare of Assassination

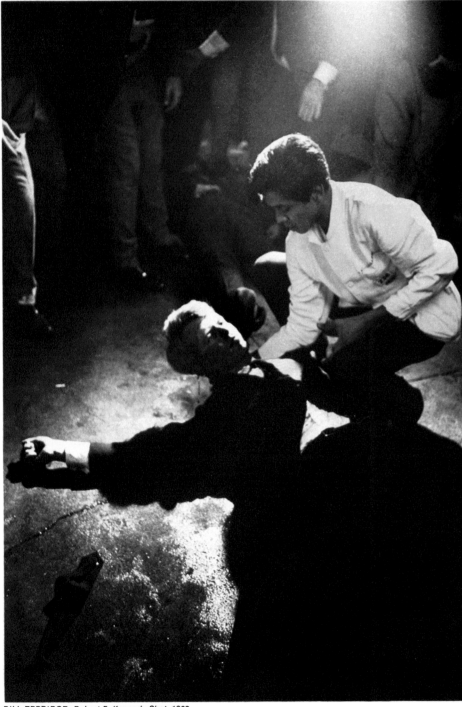

Senator Robert F. Kennedy lies in a pool of his own blood on the floor of the Ambassador Hotel in Los Angeles, semiconscious and rigid as his life ebbs away. A 24-year-old Jordanian immigrant named Sirhan Sirhan had shot him twice with a .22 caliber pistol moments after Kennedy thanked supporters for helping him win the crucial 1968 primary election in California.

Mortally wounded by a sword thrust, Inejiro ▶ Asanuma, chairman of Japan's Socialist Party, holds out his hands as if imploring his assailant —a 17-year-old ultrarightist student—not to stab him again. The vicious assassination was witnessed by 3,000 people attending a 1960 political debate in an auditorium in Tokyo.

BILL EPPRIDGE: *Robert F. Kennedy Shot, 1968*

YASUSHI NAGAO: *Inejiro Asanuma and Assassin*, 1960

The Pain of Bereavement

EDWARD CLARK: *Weeping for F.D.R.*, 1945

When Franklin D. Roosevelt, who had guided the United States through the Depression and World War II, died of a stroke at Warm Springs, Georgia, in April 1945, the sense of bereavement felt by millions was summed up in one emotion-filled picture: a weeping Navy musician, Chief Petty Officer Graham Jackson, playing Going Home as the body began the journey back to Roosevelt's home in Hyde Park, New York.

Bridging three reigns and grieving for the end of ▶ one, England's Elizabeth II, Queen Mary and the widowed Queen Consort watch as the coffin of George VI is carried into Westminster Abbey. The new Queen's father had died on February 6, 1952, after occupying the throne through 16 of the most tumultuous years in English history.

PHOTOGRAPHER UNKNOWN: *Bereaved Queens,* 1952

The Toll of War

*The blow that finally brought Japan to her knees ▶
in World War II was the destruction of the city of
Nagasaki by a single atomic bomb. Equivalent
to more than 20,000 tons of TNT, it took 35,000
lives and turned the industrial center into a
wasteland of charred rubble, as this aerial
picture by George Silk makes horrifyingly clear.*

GEORGE SILK: *Nagasaki*, 1945

H. S. ("NEWSREEL") WONG: *Chinese Baby*, 1937

Seconds after his mother was killed by Japanese bombs, a Chinese baby sits crying at a Shanghai railroad station in 1937. The attack was filmed by one of Hearst Metrotone's star newsreel photographers with a 35mm movie camera. This frame, reproduced in magazines and newspapers, stirred up international outrage at the slaughter of Chinese civilians.

During a fierce battle in the wet streets of Puerto ▶ Cabello, Venezuela, a Navy chaplain tries to aid a soldier who has been badly wounded by rebelling marines. Just after this picture was taken, the rebels sprayed a warning burst of machine-gun bullets at the feet of the chaplain, and then mercilessly finished off the soldier as he attempted to crawl out of the line of fire.

HECTOR RONDON: *Chaplain and Soldier*, 1962

The Visage of Catastrophe

ARNOLD GENTHE: *San Francisco Fire*, 1906

Distraught residents of San Francisco cluster along a rubble-strewn street, watching fire rage through the city after the earthquake of 1906. The photographer, Arnold Genthe, shared in the tragedy; his portrait studio was destroyed by the first tremor, and he lost all of his equipment and many years' worth of glass plates. Genthe borrowed a box camera to cover the holocaust, and went on to become one of the century's most notable documentary photographers.

CARL NESENSOHN: *Morro Castle Aground*, 1934

*Washed up onto a New Jersey beach in 1934, the
hulk of the luxury cruise liner Morro Castle
smolders 16 hours after the outbreak of a fire at
sea that took the lives of 134 persons.*

The Sudden Scythe of Death

Killed instantly when his speeding automobile struck a telephone pole near Cheektowaga, New York, a motorist hangs suspended in a grisly embrace of wires and crossbars. Photographer William Dyviniak recorded in one tragedy the horror of all United States highway accidents.

Plunging toward her death, a 35-year-old ▶ divorcée is frozen in the act of suicide by the camera of news photographer I. Russell Sorgi of the Buffalo Courier-Express. She had leaped from the eighth-story ledge of a hotel despite policemen's attempts to dissuade her.

WILLIAM W. DYVINIAK: *Automobile Accident,* 1945

I. RUSSELL SORGI: *Suicide*, 1942

The Law of the Gun

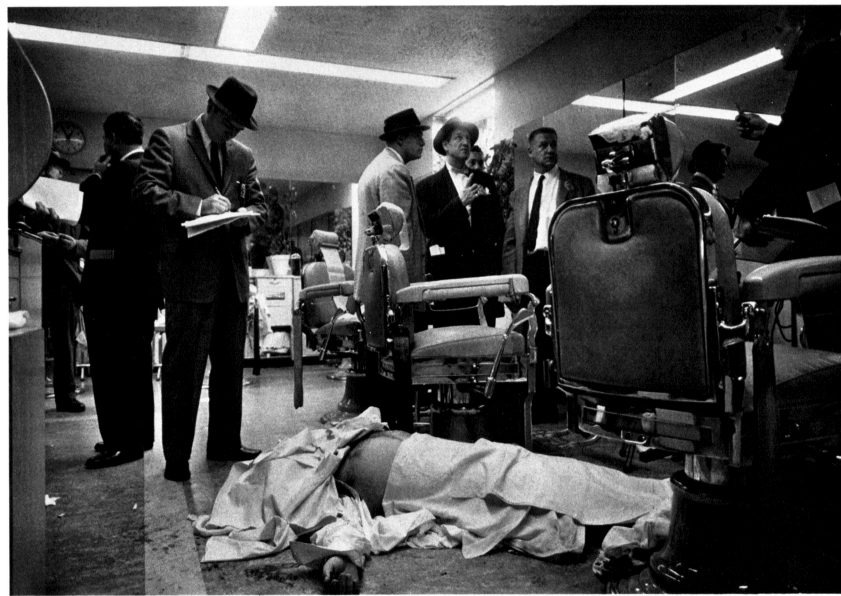

GEORGE SILK: *Detectives Inspect the Corpse of Albert Anastasia, 1957*

New York police had been trying to put Albert Anastasia behind bars for years, but it was gangster justice that finally caught up with him, as shown in LIFE photographer George Silk's picture of detectives at the scene of his slaying. Anastasia, chieftain of a Brooklyn murder ring, had been shot by fellow thugs while having his hair cut in the barber shop of the Park Sheraton.

ROGER BOCKRATH: *San Rafael Breakout*, 1970

Outside a California courthouse, a deputy surrenders to a young man, one of the two self-proclaimed revolutionaries trying to help two prisoners escape their trial in 1970. They told a photographer of the San Rafael Independence-Journal, "Take all the pictures you want," and his colleague Roger Bockrath, also covering for the Independence-Journal, recorded this part of the breakout attempt, which ended in the death of one of the prisoners, their self-appointed rescuers and the trial judge, who had been taken hostage, in a shoot-out moments later.

Bitter Struggles for Human Rights

An unknown photographer caught the fiery determination of Mrs. Emmeline Pankhurst, leader of a movement to gain voting rights for women in England, when she was arrested in front of Buckingham Palace in 1914. Although Mrs. Pankhurst was sent to jail eight times on charges of conspiracy and incitement to riot, her voice could not be stilled. British women were finally granted the vote in 1918.

PHOTOGRAPHER UNKNOWN: *The Arrest of Mrs. Pankhurst, 1914*

I. WILMER COUNTS: *Violence in Little Rock,* 1958

Heroes to the Last

NAT FEIN: *Babe Ruth Bows Out*, 1948

Fans jammed Yankee Stadium in 1948 to say goodbye to Babe Ruth, mortally ill of cancer after 22 years of matchless heroics in baseball. New York Herald Tribune photographer Nat Fein stood to the left of the Yankee bench to include in his picture members of the Babe's old team, the cheering crowd and the famed number 3 of his uniform, which was then forever retired.

MORRIS BERMAN: Y. A. Tittle, 1964

With the stunned look of a gladiator who realizes his competitive days are numbered, veteran New York Giant Y. A. Tittle kneels on the turf after a crushing tackle in 1964 by a 270-pound Pittsburgh Steeler. Tittle gamely played out the rest of the season, but it was his last.

Performances Onstage and Off

Overcome with emotion during his farewell concert in 1954, Arturo Toscanini, the great conductor of the NBC Symphony, tries to remember his place in the score. Before the last notes had been played, he dropped his baton and left the stage of Carnegie Hall, weeping.

Ignoring the scowl of a bystander, two ▶ fashionable ladies, weighted down with jewels and swathed in ermine, arrive for the opening of the 1943 Metropolitan Opera season. Because of the wartime blackout, news photographer Arthur Fellig, better known by his nickname, Weegee, was not able to see his subjects clearly. But, as he later explained, "I could smell the smugness, so I aimed the camera and made the shot."

SY FRIEDMAN: *Arturo Toscanini Retires*, 1954

WEEGEE: *The Critic*, 1943

A Wedding of Note

LISA LARSEN: *Kennedy Wedding, 1953*

*The qualities of vivacity and poise that were to
enchant millions of Americans are forever
memorialized by LIFE's Lisa Larsen as Senator
John F. Kennedy and his bride Jacqueline begin
the feast at their Newport wedding in 1953.*

Stories in Pictures **2**

ERICH SALOMON: *The Photojournalist Caught in the Act*, 1931

The Photo Essay: A New Way to Communicate

The photo essay is the most complex, and certainly one of the most interesting, end products of photography, involving as it does the use of more than one picture and the talents of more than one person—an editor in addition to the photographer, and usually a design artist as well. Like everything else in photography, it had to endure a growing-up period that was partly dependent on improvements in cameras and film, partly on a gradual realization of the potential that existed in the form itself.

Creating a photo essay requires the organization of a number of pictures on a single theme so that they give a deeper, fuller, more rounded, more intense view of their subject than any single picture could. The subject can be anything—an idea, a person, an event, a place. The organization can be either chronological or thematic; these things do not matter, since the form itself is a flexible one. What does matter is that the pictures work together to enrich the theme. They can no longer be regarded as single entities, as individual works of art, but rather as parts of a whole. For a photo essay to succeed, the whole must be greater than the sum of its parts.

There is nothing original in telling stories with pictures. This was done on Egyptian tombs and is still being done in comic strips. In photography the wherewithal for making photo essays existed as early as the work of Mathew Brady in the American Civil War, and of Roger Fenton in the Crimean War. It certainly existed in the more personalized photographs of men like John Thomson in London and Ernst Höltzer in Ottoman Persia, one of whom set out to capture the plight of the poor of his city, the other a record of a vanishing way of life.

War. People. Exotic lands. Stacks of striking photographs that explored their subjects in depth—the ingredients for magnificent picture essays. The trouble was that there was no means for reproducing them mechanically on the printing presses that turned out magazines and books so easily, and thus no realization that this fascinating new way of skewering life as it spun past could be used for the telling of stories or the development of large ideas.

Then in the 1880s and 1890s came the development of the halftone *(pages 16-17)*, a printing breakthrough that made possible for the first time fast reproduction in large quantities of any photograph. At first photographs were used singly, and even when grouped did not attempt to tell a coherent story. It was many decades before editors began to fit pictures together in a meaningful way and the photo essay—in a very primitive form—was born. These early efforts may look crude and unimpressive to modern eyes. But it should be kept in mind that the people who were doing the looking then were not swamped, as people are today, by photography and by its highly sophisticated exploitation in advertising and journalism. Like any new development, the early photo essay was a wonder of novelty and interest as long as there was nothing better to compare it to. For readers of *The Illustrated London News* during World War I, the mere presence on a page of a number of photographs on the conflict, arranged in neat cookie-cutter patterns, was fascinating. They were impressed even though the pictures, because of the bulkiness of cameras and the slowness of lenses, were mostly static shots of soldiers—sometimes posed in camps in England—and the picture arrangements did not really "go anywhere."

Then in 1925 came another breakthrough, the invention in Germany of small cameras, scarcely larger than today's 35mm, with very fast lenses. This enabled the user to take pictures unobtrusively and under low-light conditions. People were caught off guard, no longer posing for the camera but acting naturally—doing awkward, funny, dangerous, *real* things. Candid photography came into being, and with it, in German picture magazines, the first true exploitation of the potential that existed in the photo essay. It was possible now to photograph the circus in action, to explore in depth the lives of ordinary people, to peep uninvited behind the closed doors of diplomatic conferences as the pioneering photojournalist Erich Salomon did so often. (He was caught in the act once at a Paris state dinner in 1931 by French Premier Aristide Briand, who pointed an accusing finger and gave Salomon the great picture reproduced on page 53.)

The editor now became a man of great importance. It was he who sent photographers off on specific assignments, often with scripts detailing particular pictures he wanted, confident that they would come back with not just pictures but with a "story," something he could organize through skillful layout. And it was he who shaped that story by deciding which pictures he would use, and how he would use them: large, small, in sequences; for dramatic effect or for information, to inspire humor, anger, curiosity, disgust. He could not make first-class photo essays without first-class pictures, but even with them, notable essays were an impossibility unless the editor knew his business. This set up a great tension between editor and photographer—the one clamoring for better, more exciting, more "sequential" and meaningful pictures, the other moaning that his best creations were being discarded or subjected to a constricting layout. In a sense, both were right: the layout of the pictures had become nearly as important as the pictures themselves.

It was against this background that LIFE magazine was launched in 1936. In its pages, during the next two or three decades, the photo essay came into its finest flowering. The tension became more highly productive. Editor prodded photographer. Photographer responded by probing more deeply and more imaginatively into his subject. LIFE, and other magazines that followed it, took maximum advantage of every technique—in printing, photography and design—to exploit their large page size.   *Maitland Edey* ☐

A Crude Beginning in Grouped Pictures

But for the problem of printing, both of the 19th Century's pioneer war photographers, Mathew Brady and Roger Fenton, *could* have seen their work published in magazines, since each had a distinguished large-format periodical already in being to contribute to: *Harper's Weekly* in America, and *The Illustrated London News* in England. Both journals used pictures, and they would have printed photographs if they could. Instead, the photographs had to be converted to woodcuts.

When World War I broke out, the halftone process was already well developed and picture journals became voracious consumers of photographs. But the pictures were generally staged, like the one at right of a Tommy in a gas mask, which *The Illustrated London News* ran on its cover.

Photographs such as this, while they conveyed the atmosphere of war, could not capture the action; that would have to wait for faster, smaller cameras. Still, editors did the best they could, assembling spreads like the one at far right, which, with its jumble of crowds, marching troops and people waving from the tops of buses, does give an idea of the tumult of Armistice Day in London in 1918. But that is all it does. No attempt is made to tell a complete story or to emphasize a particularly good picture. All are the same size, arbitrarily arranged in an overall design that calls attention to itself, rather than to the development of any story line inherent in the pictures.

ARMISTICE DAY IN LONDON: STREET SCENES ON NOVEMBER 11 DURING THE CELEBRATION OF THE ALLIES' VICTORY.

PHOTOGRAPHS BY TOPICAL, FARRINGDON PHOTO. COMPANY, ILLUSTRATIONS BUREAU, I.N.A., C.N., AND S. AND G.

1. THE FAVOURITE METHOD OF REJOICING: FLAG-WAVING AND CHEERING MEN AND WOMEN CROWDING A MOTOR-'BUS.
2. IN THE HOUR OF VICTORY: WOMEN MILITARY MOTORISTS CELEBRATING THE SIGNING OF THE ARMISTICE.
3. ON THE CAPTURED GUNS IN THE MALL: A CHEERY CROWD OF YOUNGSTERS.
4. THE "ALL CLEAR" CAR PUT TO NEW USE: CELEBRATING THE VICTORY.
5. ANOTHER FAVOURITE METHOD OF REJOICING: A MOTOR-CAR COMMANDEERED AND CROWDED.
6. AMERICA IN THE REJOICINGS: SOLDIERS AND SAILORS IN BUCKINGHAM PALACE FORECOURT.
7. A POPULAR CAR: NURSES AND WOUNDED SOLDIERS.
8. CHEERING THE PRIME MINISTER: THE CROWD IN DOWNING STREET.
9. DRIVING IN TRIUMPH: HOSPITAL-WORKERS DEMONSTRATING.
10. TAKING THE KAISER TO COVER: A POPULAR CARTOON.
11. A RALLYING POINT: DEMONSTRATING ROUND A WOUNDED SOLDIER.
12. FLAG-WAGGING ON ARMISTICE DAY: WOMEN OF THE W.R.A.F.

London broke into a spontaneous outburst of joy on that memorable Monday morning (November 11, 1918) when it learned "the greatest piece of news that England has ever heard," the announcement that Germany had accepted and signed the terms of the armistice, and that hostilities ceased on that day. The reaction of relief after four years of strain and anxiety had its natural result. The long-pent feelings of a people which, throughout the war, had never indulged in jubilations over incidental successes, found expression at last in the hour of final triumph. London quickly became the scene of an improvised carnival. Happy crowds thronged the streets cheering, singing, waving, and wearing innumerable flags. Vehicles of all sorts—omnibuses, lorries, vans, and taxi-cabs—were crowded to overflowing with vociferous humanity; windows and balconies were filled with bunting and spectators. Amid all the noise and high spirits, however, there was nothing unseemly or indecorous, but beneath the surface ran an undercurrent of deep and solemn thanksgiving. The Prime Minister expressed the prevailing mood in the few words he spoke to the crowd from his windows in Downing Street. "You are entitled to rejoice," he said. "The people of this country and the people of the Dominions and of our Allies have won such a victory for freedom as the world has never seen. You have all had a share in it. Sons and daughters of the people have done it, and this is their hour for rejoicing."

Fast Cameras Make the Essay Possible

The new candid cameras, the Ermanox and the more convenient Leica that was developed a short time afterward, were both products of the German camera industry, and their impact was first felt in German picture magazines, notably the *Münchner Illustrierte Presse* (Munich Illustrated Press). Its editor, a Hungarian-born innovator named Stefan Lorant, seized on the opportunity of the new action pictures produced by the new cameras to convey to his readers a sense of that action—of being there. He also took some bold steps in the direction of further enhancing the effectiveness of these pictures by skillful contrasts in size, mood and organization in their layout on two facing pages, the unit of design that has become basic to all illustrated journalism. His spread on a circus *(above),* made in 1929, shows these forces crudely at work. A candid shot of the people in the crowd straining their necks at high-wire performers pulls the reader into the scene, while more action is detailed in the strip at left. Slower cameras simply could not have produced such pictures, nor given Lorant the chance to use them boldly to tell his sharply realized little stories.

...with the Help of Effective Layouts

In contrast to the circus spread of the preceding page, here are different pictures and an entirely different mood, but once again a deliberate attempt has been made to organize photographs into something more than just a collection of snapshots. These men are all members of the German Reichstag, shot off guard, cupping their ears, looking bored, exhausted—in short, public figures as they really were, but as they had never before been seen by the public. The magazine is again the *Münchner Illustrierte Presse,* the year is 1929, the editor is again Stefan Lorant. His layout is jagged and ugly, deliberately so in an effort to intensify the mood he was after: a sense of being right there in the chamber, hit by all the crosscurrents of disputation, thought, personality and prejudice that confuse men trying to run a country. Both these spreads show an advance over *The Illustrated London News* example. Each has taken the bold step of using pictures, not merely in patterns, but in ways calculated to enhance the special quality of the pictures themselves. This step was fundamental to the further development of the photo essay.

Penetrating the Strongholds of the Great

After a stretch in a Nazi concentration camp, Lorant slipped out of Germany in 1934 and made his way to England, where he further refined his techniques in the London *Weekly Illustrated.* In the company of the photographer Felix Man, he had called on Mussolini three years earlier and obtained a series of exclusive pictures of Il Duce in his private offices. (Lorant is the figure, back to camera, talking to the dictator by the fireplace at right above.) The pictures had been published in the *Münchner Illustrierte Presse;* now Lorant presented them to the English-reading public, providing an actual behind-the-scenes visit to the notorious dictator about whose personality and life style the entire world was curious. Both are swiftly captured in the pictures Lorant selected: in the awesome decor of his working quarters, and in the close-in head shots of the man at work. With a story as powerful as this one, Lorant very properly used a much more sober layout style than he had used in the two examples previously shown.

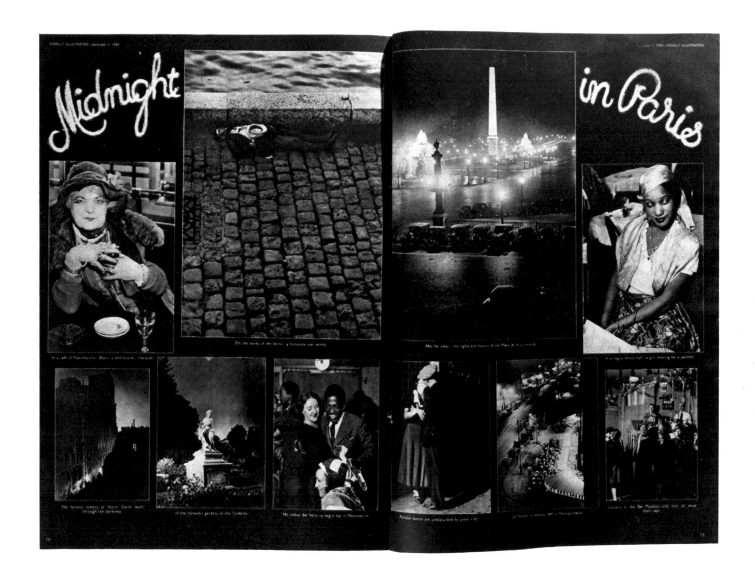

Still experimenting and still developing, Lorant created this glimpse of Paris at night for the London *Weekly Illustrated* in 1934. By employing an overall dark background he not only strengthened the mood of his story but he was also able to hold its various bits together much better than he had in his circus spread *(page 58),* even though its ele-ments are more varied and the layout problem is correspondingly more difficult. The photographer is the Hungarian-born Brassaï, whose sensitive eye roamed from monument to nightclub entertainer, from aging tart to cobbled gutter, as he slowly built up, picture by picture, enough pieces to tell a small evocative story about a single place.

61

The Photo Essay Comes of Age

The photojournalistic techniques pioneered by Stefan Lorant galvanized the American publishers, particularly when, during the 1930s, some of the best German photographers he had been using came to the United States to avoid persecution by Hitler. The times were right for the launching of an American picture magazine, and by the middle of the decade groups of editors in several companies were hard at work preparing dummies. In 1936 one such group wrote the most famous declaration of intent that has ever been articulated for a magazine:

"To see life; to see the world; to eyewitness great events; to watch the faces of the poor and the gestures of the proud; to see strange things—machines, armies, multitudes, shadows in the jungle and on the moon; to see man's work—his paintings, towers and discoveries; to see things thousands of miles away, things hidden behind walls and within rooms, things dangerous to come to; the women that men love and many children; to see and take pleasure in seeing; to see and be amazed; to see and be instructed."

This was the manifesto for LIFE, whose first issue was on the stands in November 1936. Its success surprised even its editors. Within months it was followed by *Look, See, Photo, Picture, Focus, Pic* and *Click,* to name some that tried to ride the huge but uneasy

breaker of pictorial journalism. Only LIFE and *Look* survived.

For its first cover LIFE assigned Margaret Bourke-White, then known chiefly as an architectural photographer, to make a picture of the Fort Peck Dam, which was being built in Montana. She made her cover *(right),* but she also stayed on to record something else. Around Fort Peck had sprung up a cluster of shanty settlements with their false fronts and dusty rutted streets, their tough migrant workers and scruffy taxi dancers thronging the bars on Saturday nights. Here was something that Americans had not seen for many years —a glimpse of the frontier suddenly reopened. The LIFE editor in charge, John Shaw Billings, spotted the potential in Bourke-White's pictures—the "take" in photojournalists' jargon. And in that first issue of LIFE he laid out the first photo essay in the form known today—organizing several subelements within an overall theme. He emerged not with a small group of pictures but with nine pages of them, shaped into a coherent picture story. The first page of the essay is at far right; two other spreads are shown on pages 64-65.

In the years that followed, LIFE delivered on all of the promises listed in its manifesto—including pictures of shadows taken on the moon—and in the process developed the photo essay to limits undreamed of by its pioneers.

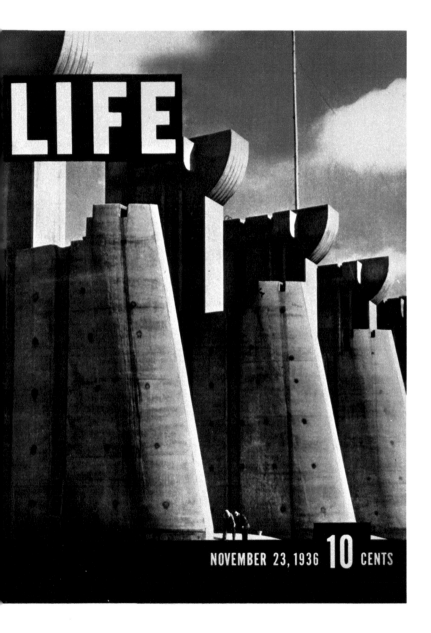

LIFE

NOVEMBER 23, 1936 **10** CENTS

VOL. 1, NO. 1 **LIFE** NOV. 23, 1936

10,000 MONTANA RELIEF WORKERS MAKE WHOOPEE ON SATURDAY NIGHT

THE frontier has returned to the cow country. But not with cows. In the shanty towns which have grown up around the great U. S. work-relief project at Fort Peck, Montana, there are neither long-horns nor lariats. But there is about everything else the West once knew with the exception of the two-gun shootings; the bad men of the shanty towns are the modern gangster type of gun-waver. The saloons are as wide open as the old Bull's Head at Abilene. The drinks are as raw as they ever were at Uncle Ben Dowell's. If the hombres aren't as tough as Billy the Kid they are tough enough—particularly on pay day. Even the dancing has the old Cheyenne flavor. These taxi-dancers with the chuffed and dusty shoes lope around with their fares in something half way between the old barroom stomp and the lackadaisical stroll of the college boys at Roseland. They will lope all night for a nickel a number. Pay is on the rebate system. The fare buys his lady a five cent beer for a dime. She drinks the beer and the management refunds the nickel. If she can hold sixty beers she makes three dollars—and frequently she does.

Nov. 23rd

9

THE NEW WEST'S NEW HOTSPOT IS A TOWN CALLED "NEW DEAL"

THE COW TOWNS THAT GET........THEIR MILK FROM KEGS

A relief project started the new Wild West. But you don't need a government loan to build a house there. For $2 a month you can rent a fifty foot lot in Wheeler from Joe Frazier, the barber over in Glasgow, 20 miles away. Joe had the fool luck to homestead the worthless land on which shanty towns have sprouted. You then haul in a load of grocer's boxes, tin cans, crazy doors and building paper and knock your shack together. That will set you back $40 to $75 more. You then try to live in it in weather which can hit minus 50° one way and plus 110° the other.

Water in the cities of the new Wild West comes from wells, many of them shallow, some condemned—and at that it may cost you a cent a gallon. Sewage disposal is by the Chic Sale system. Compulsory typhoid inoculation is non-existent. Fires are frequent—Wheeler has had 20 more or less this year. Nevertheless the workers here refuse to move to the Army's sanitary barracks. Life in barracks is too expensive; life in the shanty towns too gay. When the Army tried compulsion they wrote to Montana's Senator Wheeler for whom their metropolis was named. They won.

UNCLE SAM TAKES CARE OF THE INDIANS: THE LITTLE LADY, HERSELF.

THE ONLY IDLE BEDSPRINGS IN "NEW DEAL" ARE THE BROKEN ONES

LIFE IN THE COWLESS COW TOWNS IS LUSH BUT NOT CHEAP.

THE pioneer mother can trek in broken-down Fords as well as in covered wagons. And she can crack her hands in the alkali water of 1936 as quickly as in the alkali water of 1849. When the Fort Peck project opened in 1933 the roads of Montana began to rattle with second-hand cars full of children, chairs, mattresses and tired women. Most of them kept right on rattling toward some other hopeless hope. Some of them parked in the shanty towns around Fort Peck. There, their women passengers got jobs like Mrs. Nelson (*right*) who washes New Deal without running water, or tried their feet at taxi-dancing like the girls on the preceding pages, or made money like Ruby Smith on page 15, or gave birth to children in zero weather in a crowded 8 by 16-foot shack like many an unnamed woman of New Deal and Wheeler. The girl at the bar (*above*) who works as a waitress ("hasher") takes her child to work with her because she can't leave her at home. She sits on the bar while her mother kids with the customers. The group on the right, it will be noticed, resembles a statue recently erected to the Pioneer Mother of the old frontier. No statues are expected at New Deal.

MONTANA SATURDAY NIGHTS: FINIS

For the First Time: War as It Really Is

The birth of new picture magazines was not limited to America. In 1938 *Picture Post* made its debut in London. Its editor: Stefan Lorant. One of his first acts was to assign a young fellow-Hungarian, Robert Capa, to cover the war in Spain. Capa proved to be a superb photojournalist. He had a great photographic eye, enormous personal daring and a tough, swaggering panache. He spent these recklessly, covering five wars and becoming a photojournalistic legend during his short life.

All that Capa would become is discernible in his first Spanish War take, part of which is shown here—a counterattack by government troops along the Ebro River in the fall of 1938. It is light-years away from the World War I spread shown on pages 56-57. To begin with, it tells a story, each picture numbered to make sure that the reader follows its thread. It opens almost like a play, with a briefing in a dugout. The men are not posing for the photographer; they are oblivious of him, too busy to notice him, their faces strained by anxiety and fatigue. The action now speedily builds up: the commander makes a speech to his men, weapons

are lugged into position, and actual fighting starts. Capa is there in the center of it all, catching the jar of an exploding shell, the stumbling rush of a prisoner being led to the rear, the dust, the confusion.

"If your pictures aren't good enough, you aren't close enough," Capa once said. This was war photography of a new kind, to be practiced by other photographers with increasing grimness and vividness in all the wars that followed. Capa himself continued to get close, swam ashore with the first assault wave of American troops in Normandy on D-Day, making unforgettable pictures for LIFE of men struggling and dying in the water. Predictably his own life was ended by a land mine in Indochina in 1954.

An Ordinary Life Examined in Depth

Many photographers honed their talents on the whetstone of World War II. One of the youngest and ablest of them was Leonard McCombe, an Englishman who became a member of the LIFE staff in 1945 at the age of 22. He had already been a professional photographer for four years.

McCombe's association with LIFE proved to be pivotal for the photo essay. With the war over, there was an intense desire on the part of everybody to return to the plain business of living and a corresponding demand for picture stories about just plain people. McCombe's special skill lay in his ability to involve himself closely with such people *(pages 172-190)*, sticking with them round the clock, photographing everything they did—until finally they became oblivious of his presence and began laying bare all the turmoil, the strains and joys, the bitter moments and the tender ones that go to make up any life. His photo essay on Gwyned Filling, a young college girl trying to make a start on an advertising career in New York, is an acknowledged masterpiece in this genre.

When McCombe and LIFE editor Joseph J. Thorndike got through with the young career girl, there was nothing about her and her life in New York that the reader did not feel he knew. After 12 pages of intimate pictures Gwyned Filling was as vividly real as a sister, a daughter or even a wife.

GWYNED FILLING, ALONE IN A CROWD THAT HAS GATHERED TO WATCH A FIRE IN THE CITY, STANDS ON TIPTOE AND TILTS BACK HER HEAD TO GET A BETTER VIEW

THE PRIVATE LIFE OF

Gwyned Filling

THE HOPES AND FEARS OF COUNTLESS YOUNG CAREER GIRLS ARE SUMMED UP IN HER STRUGGLE TO SUCCEED IN NEW YORK

PHOTOGRAPHS FOR LIFE BY LEONARD McCOMBE

In the spring of 1925 in St. Charles, Mo., a housewife named Mildred Filling picked up a newspaper and saw in the society column an odd first name: Gwyned. Because Mrs. Filling was about to have a child, this solved the christening problem, and it now accounts for the fact that an attractive 23-year-old girl alone among the crowds of New York would stop and turn if that odd name were spoken.

Gwyned Filling came to New York last June to begin a career. Because she wanted to feel independent she had borrowed $250 from a local bank rather than from her father, a former city official. She had a large ambition and some training, having just completed a course in advertising at the University of Missouri. With her came her college roommate, Marilyn Johnson, who had taken the same course. For

five weeks they looked unsuccessfully for jobs, during which Gwyned's $250 shriveled to $30. But finally she walked down the right street, took the right elevator and entered the offices of Newell-Emmett Co., a large advertising agency which handles the account for Chesterfield cigarets. Gwyned was hired for $35 a week, which disappears quickly in New York.

Because she had already worked her way through college and had learned to make her clothes and to eat breakfast for 15¢, Gwyned got along. With Marilyn, she found an 11x15-foot furnished room in an apartment building on 23rd Street. Although they could scarcely afford the stiff $75-a-month rent, they could find nothing cheaper. Gwyned soon made office friends, including several young men who began to take her out to dinner regularly enough to subtract

about $4 a week from her living expenses. An older couple turned over their apartment, empty on weekends, to both girls. This saves no money, but it is a release from the drab clutter of their single room.

After six months Gwyned's salary was raised to $52 a week. She commenced, unoer careful supervision, to write fragments of advertising copy. She also began to repay, at the rate of $21.93 a month, her borrowed $250.

Gwyned's life is interesting and often gay, but beneath the gaiety lie the problems which confront all career girls. How much of her time and nerves must she sacrifice for success? When should she marry, and will she jeopardize her chance by trying to close her eyes to everything but her career? Gwyned has no ready answer, but even as she works she knows she must find one.

CONTINUED ON NEXT PAGE 103

HER DAY BEGINS WITH A FRANTIC   RACE AGAINST THE CLOCK

Gwyned has two alarm clocks. Both of them are broken, and thus at 7:30 she is roused by her landlady, Mrs. Bell. Even after 10 months in New York, Gwyned is still occasionally surprised to wake and find herself far from home in a small room and glances hastily across at Marilyn to make certain her friend is there.

Marilyn and Gwyned take their morning baths hurriedly according to a strict rotation schedule, each having the tub first on alternate days. The other placidly waits her turn and reads aloud inconsequential items from the St. Charles *Cosmos-Monitor*, which is mailed to them daily and remains a firm link with home.

Breakfast is eaten hastily in a restaurant across the street. The 15¢ meal consists of two slices of toast and a cup of coffee. Gladys Hallem, the counter girl, invariably greets Gwyned with, "How are things in St. Charles, Mo. today, baby?" and then gets the girls' food quickly because she already knows what they will order.

After breakfast the girls race for the bus, which takes them eastward along 23rd Street to Fourth Avenue. Sometimes, when Gwyned is in an economical mood, either by choice or circumstance, she rises half an hour early and walks—or trots —17 blocks to the office, a distance of about a mile. The terrible aimless urgency

for speed, which affects all of New York, has already taken hold of Gwyned and Marilyn. Even though another bus will be along within two minutes, the girls scramble down the rain-soaked street, splattering their shoes and stockings with water and grime, in order to make sure they will not be left behind by this one.

When she reaches the office at 9, after her frantic dash to get there on time, Gwyned must often wait patiently until her boss has time to see her. Waiting with her is George Flanagan, a copy supervisor who occasionally supplies reassurance about her work while she musters up courage to show it to her department head.

CONTINUED ON NEXT PAGE

The Photo Essay Comes of Age: continued

CAREER GIRL CONTINUED

Gwyned at 23 has been in love only once, and then briefly—a high-school engagement was quietly called off when she and her fiancé changed their minds. In New York she meets a number of young men who are attracted to her. She has two office acquaintances—Carl Nichols (*above*) and Charles Straus (*p. 112*)—who are handicapped by the fact that they are in professional competition with her. Also, she has made many sacrifices to begin her career and has accordingly surrounded herself with a kind of protective insulation. Even when she is lonely she insists that she wants to work for at least five more years. One evening with Carl she saw a small stuffed cat in a store window. It was a charming toy. Carl bought it for her. Now she is very fond of it and keeps it in her room and silly picks it up and pets it from time to time. She remembers that evening not so much because of what Carl said or how he looked, but because it was the night she acquired the cat.

SOMETIMES HER LIFE IS LIGHT AND GAY...

George Fowler is one of Newell-Emmett's eight partners, part of whose job is to maintain cordial relations between the company and its more important clients. He and his wife have in a sense adopted Gwyned, inviting her out to their country home in New Jersey for weekends. The Fowlers see in Gwyned many of the qualities of their own daughters. Mr. Fowler is full of friendly advice, warning and advising her about how to succeed without offending others in the firm. Recently he wrote a long *Ode to Gwyned's Parents*, which he forwarded to the surprised Fillings in Missouri.

One of the brightest spots in Gwyned's New York life is her relationship with Pierre (*second from left*) and Betty Duquesne (*p. 106*), whose large walk-up apartment she occupies on weekends while they are out of town. At the Duquesnes' frequent parties Gwyned is vivacious and carefree among people she might otherwise never encounter: artists and illustrators, musicians and writers. For a few hours she is able to forget the tension of the office and the urgency of her career—there will be time to worry about it in the morning. She laughs easily and adjusts readily to new groups.

110

CONTINUED ON NEXT PAGE 111

. . . AND SOMETIMES SHE CRIES

Gwyned has a deep curiosity about New Yorkers and how they behave. Walking about the city she stops when she comes upon one of the street rallies which go on daily. Here she attends a Zionist demonstration, listening with attention because anti-Semitism and Palestine are major topics among her friends.

Gwyned's favorite beau is Charles Straus, with whom she becomes more moody than with others. Charlie is shy and quiet but shows flashes of wit which Gwyned likes and is extremely capable in his copywriting job. Often he quotes long random passages of verse and laughs at Gwyned when she tries and fails to identify them. However, his shyness sometimes irritates her. Despite her wariness of emotional entanglements at this early stage in her career, she occasionally feels a need for masculine reassurance and sympathy. Idly she touches his wrist with her finger while Charlie talks of something far away.

Gwyned's boyfriends sometimes get a sly going-over at morning gossip sessions in the office. Another subject which is brought up around the coffeepot, presided over by Gwyned's office mate Margery Paddock (left), is Gwyned's quick rise from $35 to $52 a week. "You've been here 10 months, Gwyned? Strange, it seems much less. Now, that intelligent, talented Miss Jones down the hall . . . she's been here over two years, and I wonder when they'll give *her* a chance to write some copy. . . ." The gossip does not much disturb Gwyned, who has long since learned to take it as an inevitable by-product of office competition.

After a telephone squabble with Charlie, Gwyned bursts into tears on Marilyn's shoulder. The events which lead up to one of these rare outbursts are as a rule inconsequential. Gwyned is under continual strain because she is anxious to make a success of her career. Tears might be caused merely by the shattering of a tumbler or a cigaret burn on a new dress. In this case it was the simple and harmless vagueness of Charlie Straus. For some time it had been his habit to take her out only on weekends. Therefore she looked forward to such times. On Saturday morning he telephoned but mentioned nothing of his plans for the evening. Later another friend called her, and in annoyance she accepted his invitation to dinner. When Charlie at length telephoned again, this time with a definite plan, it was too late. Gwyned, weeping on Marilyn's shoulder, said she would never speak to him again. She spoke to him again bright and early on Monday morning in the office.

CONTINUED ON NEXT PAGE

The Classic Essay

One of the most brilliant war photographers was the moody young genius W. Eugene Smith, who covered the conflict in the Pacific for LIFE and returned home with large parts of his face shattered by shellfire. In time he was well enough to work again, and he began turning out picture essays that, for their intensity and photographic beauty, are still unsurpassed. Smith's own favorite among all his essays is one on a Negro midwife working in the back country of North Carolina—"In many ways it was the most rewarding experience photography has allowed me," he says—but by the judgment of most the palm should go to his "Spanish Village," shot in 1951 and shown here in its entirety.

The mood of "Spanish Village" is totally different from McCombe's story on Gwyned Filling. One concentrates on an individual, the other one on life itself. Smith's villagers, in these extraordinary pictures, are clearly individuals, yet they are more than that; they stand for all of mankind—ground down clean and pure and recognizable as archetypes of us all.

120

ON THE OUTSKIRTS

At midmorning the sun beats down on clustered stone houses. In the distance is belfry of Deleitosa's church.

Spanish Village

IT LIVES IN ANCIENT POVERTY AND FAITH

The village of Deleitosa, a place of about 2,300 peasant people, sits on the high, dry, western Spanish tableland called Estremadura, about halfway between Madrid and the border of Portugal. Its name means "delightful," which it no longer is, and its origins are obscure, though they may go back a thousand years to Spain's Moorish period. In any event it is very old and Life Photographer Eugene Smith, wandering off the main road into the village, found that its ways had advanced little since medieval times.

Many Deleitosans have never seen a railroad because the nearest one is 25 miles away. The Madrid-Sevilla highway passes Deleitosa seven miles to the north, so almost the only automobiles it sees are a dilapidated sedan and an old station wagon, for hire at prices few villagers can afford. Mail comes in by burro. The nearest telephone is 12½ miles away in another town. Deleitosa's water system still consists of the sort of aqueducts and open wells from which villagers have drawn their water for centuries. Except for the local doctor's portable tin bathtub there is no trace of any modern sanitation, and the streets smell strongly of the villagers' donkeys and pigs.

There are a few signs of the encroachment of the 20th Century in Deleitosa. In the city hall, which is run by political subordinates of the provincial governor, one typewriter clatters. A handful of villagers, including the mayor, own their own small radio sets. About half of the 800 homes of the village are dimly lighted after dark by weak electric-light bulbs which dangle from ancient ceilings. And a small movie theater, which shows some American films, sits among the sprinkling of little shops near the main square. But the village scene is dominated now as always by the high, brown structure of the 16th Century church, the center of society in Catholic Deleitosa. And the lives of the villagers are dominated as always by the bare and brutal problems of subsistence. For Deleitosa, barren of history, unfavored by nature, reduced by wars, lives in poverty—a poverty shared by nearly all and relieved only by the seasonal work of the soil, and the faith that sustains most Deleitosans from the hour of First Communion (*opposite page*) until the simple funeral (*pp. 128, 129*) that marks one's end.

PHOTOGRAPHED FOR LIFE BY W. EUGENE SMITH

FIRST COMMUNION DRESS

Lorenza Curiel, 7, is a sight for her young neighbors as she waits for her mother to lock door, take her to church.

"EL MEDICO"

Dr. José Martin makes rounds with lantern to light patients' homes. He does minor surgery, sending serious cases to city of Cáceres, and treats much typhus.

MALL BOY'S WORK

ungest son in the Curiel family,
old Lutero, sweeps up manure
e street outside his home. It is
y hoarded as fertilizer, will be
a the eight small fields the fam-
s or rents a few miles out of town.

"SENOR CURA"

n a walk, the village priest. Don
el, 69, passes barred window and
ned door of a home. He has seldom
ed in politics—the village was
ily split during the civil war—but
to ministry. Villagers like that.

YOUNG WOMAN'S WORK

ero Curiel's big sister Bernardina,
kicks open door of community oven,
ch the village provides for public
At least once a week she bakes 24
es for the family of eight. The flour
es from family grain, ground locally.

Spanish Village CONTINUED

DIVIDING THE GROUND

At harvesttime many of the villagers bring unthreshed wheat from their outlying fields to a large public field next to town. Here they stake out 5-by-12-yard plots where they spread the full stalks, thresh grain as forefathers did.

HAGGLING OVER LOTS

Sometimes luck gives one family stony ground for threshing, another smooth. This brings arguments since the smooth ground makes for easier threshing—a process begun by driving burros over stalks with a drag that loosens kernels.

SEEDING TIME

Beans planted, the villager presses hard on his flattened plow as it scrapes the dry soil back into furrows. A neighbor woman leads donkeys, one borrowed.

PLOWBOY FOR HIRE

Genaro Curiel, 17, son of man planting beans (*above*), carries his crude wooden plow as he heads for work at a wage of 12 pesetas (30¢) and one meal a day.

WINNOWING GRAIN

With the straw already broken away, wheat kernels are swept into a pile and one of the women threshers tosses them up so the breeze can carry off the chaff.

CONTINUED ON NEXT PAGE **125**

GUARDIA CIVIL.

These stern men, enforcers of national law, are Franco's rural police. They patrol countryside, are feared by people in villages, which also have local police.

VILLAGE SCHOOL

Girls are taught in separate classes from the boys. Four rooms and four lay teachers handle all pupils, as many as 300 in winter, between the ages of 6 and 14.

◄ **FAMILY DINNER**

The Curiels eat thick bean and potato soup from common pot on dirt floor of their kitchen. The father, mother and four children all share the one bedroom.

126

A CHRISTENING

While his godfather holds him over a font, the priest Don Manuel dries the head of month-old Buenaventura Jimenez Morena after his baptism at village church.

THE THREAD MAKER

A peasant woman moistens the fibers of locally grown flax as she joins them in a long strand which is spun tight by the spindle (*right*), then wrapped around it.

CONTINUED ON NEXT PAGE 127

Spanish Village CONTINUED

128

HIS WIFE, DAUGHTER, GRANDDAUGHTER AND FRIENDS
HAVE THEIR LAST EARTHLY VISIT WITH A VILLAGER

129

Exploring the World of the Social Outcast

'We are animals in a world no one knows'

A LIFE SERIES IN TWO PARTS

Pretty girl named Karen, pleasant young man named John—they could be hurrying to a movie, a supermarket, a college classroom. But they are drug addicts, headed for heroin, for a pusher with a fix. This series, reported and written by Associate Editor James Mills, tells what their lives are like and, in next week's instalment, what more could be done—to help the addict, to halt the flow of drugs and to clean up a tragic and tenacious social evil.

Photographed by BILL EPPRIDGE

If ordinary lives can produce drama in photo essays, why cannot extraordinary ones produce more? This question has led photographers into many seamy corners of crime, social injustice and decay. In 1965, when the drug problem was still largely unknown to the bulk of Americans, LIFE shocked its readers with an incisive two-part essay on a couple of youthful heroin addicts, photographed by Bill Eppridge. Eppridge followed the McCombe technique of round-the-clock intimate observation of two attractive, apparently normal young people whose private lives were a careening horror. His pictures catch the mood. They are raw, nervous, full of twitchy movement and desperate emotion—most of them shot in a hard, uncompromising light, a glare straight from hell. ☐

John out of jail: 'Don't play with my brains!'

Meeting Karen his first day out of jail (above), John bawls her out for not writing. Later in a hotel (below) he gets affectionate, his drug-free days in jail having restored desires dulled by heroin.

Go ahead and shoot it all up! You're a pig junky, just like you always were and always will be!" Karen screams at John as he takes a shot (above) minutes after his release from jail. Before he was arrested he had hidden 30 bags of heroin in a hotel hallway. Just after meeting Karen, he retrieved his stash, collected some friends and went to another hotel to "turn everyone on" —give them all heroin. In jail, off heroin, his body lost its dependence on the drug, and he uses it here not to fight off withdrawal, but only to get a high. But Karen still has a physical need for the drug and is furious at him for not giving it all to her. He shouted back at her, "Don't bug me, Karen! Don't play with my brains!" All 30 bags were gone by that night. A friend went for more and returned with a connection from Harlem, whom Karen paid off (right). Frightened that the men in the room were about to rob him of his drugs and money, the pusher was in a rush to get paid and did not complain about being photographed. Nevertheless, since his identification might encourage him to retaliate against John and Karen, his face has been retouched.

70

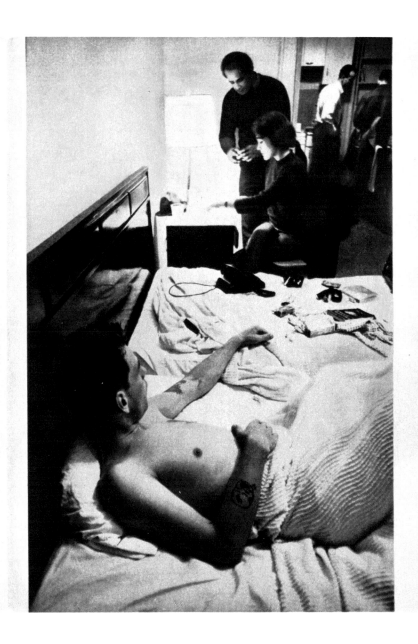

83

The deadly overdose: 'You got to fight it, Billy!'

One of the junky's natural enemies is the overdose, the "OD"—a shot that unexpectedly contains more heroin than his body can survive. In these pictures, taken while Johnny was in jail, Karen works to save the life of a young addict named Billy. Her expressions (right) mirror the danger, hope and final victory of her two-hour struggle. Billy collapsed in a hotel room after swallowing five Doriden tablets and then mainlining a shot of heroin. Though he is nearly unconscious, Karen holds him on his feet and keeps him walking.

"Open your eyes, Billy. Try to wake up. You took too much stuff, Billy. Don't go to sleep—you might not wake up. You got to fight it, Billy. Do you hear me, Billy? Billy? You got to fight it, Billy!" Exhausted and hot from walking him around the room, Karen has dumped him into a chair and removed her sweater. Then, afraid that if he sits down too long he will slip into a fatal coma, she walks him some more. Finally, she sits him down in a chair again and shouts into his ear. He begins to come around. "That Doriden is something," she explains. "It makes you feel like you were almost clean, almost like you'd never had any heroin before. And then you take the heroin and, man, it really sends you."

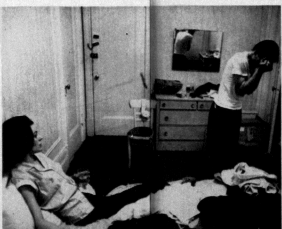

Still only half-conscious, Billy sits with a cigaret in his hand and a wet towel thrown over his neck. Now that he can walk by himself, Karen—who herself has had a shot of heroin—rests on the bed with a glass of water. Billy begins to mumble, finally gets out a complete sentence: "Man, that was a good bag." He was lucky it wasn't better. Almost every day in New York City an addict dies of an overdose, some sold intentionally by pushers who think the addict has been "stooling" to detectives. Sometimes these "hotshots" contain no heroin at all, but rat poison. Addicts call this type of hotshot a "ten-cent pistol" because the poison costs a dime but is as effective as a gun. Junkies may be quite informal about disposing of OD'd friends. Karen once heard a strange sound ("it was like shhhhh, shhhhh") outside her hotel room. When she looked she saw two junkies dragging a body down the hall.

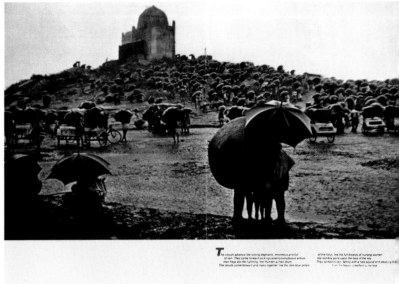

Sullen clouds are gathering fast over the black fringe of the forest
The rain water is running in rills through the narrow lanes
like a laughing boy who has run away from his mother to tease her
The sky seems to ride fast upon the madly rushing rain. the water
in the river is loud and impatient. women have hastened home early
from the Ganges with their filled pitchers
The wind is roaring and struggling.   like a wild beast tangled in a net
From the Rainy Day by Rabindranath Tagore

The clouds advance like rutting elephants. enormous and full
of rain. They come forward as kings among tumultuous armies.
their flags are the lightning. the thunder is their drum
The clouds come forward and mass together like the dark blue petals
of the lotus. like the full breasts of nursing women.
like sombre paint upon the face of the sky
They spread in rain. falling with a new sound and pleasing the
From the Season of the Rains by Kalidasa

Voici venu le temps de la
grande souffrance du Punjab.
Il n'y a plus un souffle de vent. Les arbrisseaux
sont inertes, les arbres dépouillés.
Parmi les seuls rescapés : les flamboyants et
les acajous. Les paysans hagards
cherchent le salut dans
les dernières ombrages. Dans les villes,
d'innombrables paysans indigents
la progression de
la mousson. On peut prévoir une
saison pré-Goanal, sur les panneaux, le
quartiers des pluies est ressuscité par un templier
les visages ravagés se tournent
vers le ciel dans l'espoir de la grande

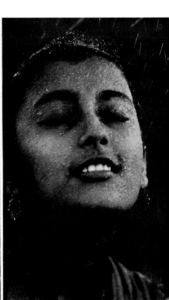

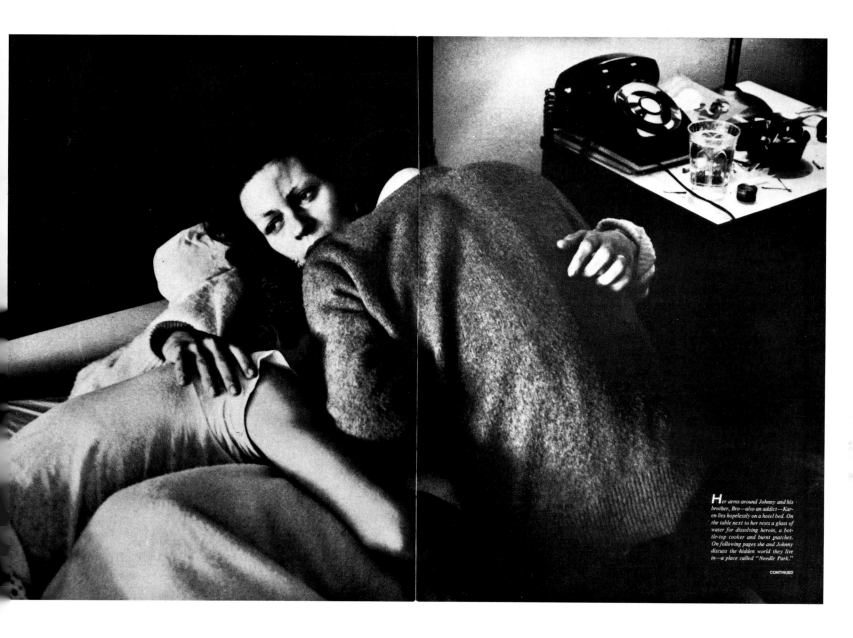

Her arms around Johnny and his brother, Bro—also an addict—Karen lies hopelessly on a hotel bed. On the table next to her rests a glass of water for dissolving heroin, a bottle-top cooker and burnt matches. On following pages she and Johnny discuss the hidden world they live in—a place called "Needle Park."

CONTINUED

The Photo Essay and the Design Artist

The preceding pages have traced the growth of the photo essay from "just pictures" assembled any which way, through small editorial ideas realized by photographers to larger ones, to the final emergence of a distinct art form of great editorial complexity and sometimes profound emotional and esthetic impact. At the peak to which it was brought by Leonard McCombe and W. Eugene Smith, the photo essay was strongly influenced by "story"; thus in its published form it necessarily reflected the ideas and tastes of the editor who commissioned it and saw it to press. For the present, certainly, the photo essay seems to have gone about as far as it can in the direction of story dictating choice of photographs. Recently the trend has been toward a return to the purely pictorial elements of a story, and frequently the shaping hand in the editor's office has been that of the designer, the graphic artist responsible for the appearance of the completed layout. A fine example of this may be found in Brian Brake's exquisite essay on an Indian monsoon.

There is not much intellectual content in Brake's pictures, and only the sketchiest kind of a story line—the suggestion of seasonal cycle: destructive drought, redeeming rain. What they do have is mood and beauty; they are drenched with both. It is up to the designer to extract as much of both as he can through emphasis on the most atmospheric pictures in his layout.

Brake's pictures so attracted editors that they were published in four picture magazines: LIFE in the U.S., *Paris-Match* in France, *Queen* in England, and *Epoca* in Italy. In 1965 the Museum of Modern Art in New York had an ex- hibition that included the four different layout treatments of the same set of pictures. Two of those treatments, one made for LIFE and another for *Paris-Match,* are partially shown overleaf; the LIFE layout lacks two spreads, the *Match* layout lacks one.

When one considers the almost limitless number of possibilities—Brake's take included more than 500 shots and 110 were offered to LIFE—what seems remarkable is that the different designers ended up with stories that were very much alike. They did not choose exactly the same pictures but they almost did, as the sampling shows.

Is this so remarkable? Not really, not even that identical pictures were chosen by LIFE and *Match* for full pages or double spreads, or that each designer chose the same opening photograph and the same ender. Photographs of transcendent beauty or originality will assert their claim on any skilled designer, as will the logic of their ideas. In short, the photographer—by what he does, by the kinds of pictures he delivers—can affect the ultimate layout of a photo essay more strongly than most photographers will admit.

The 22 pictures at right were all used in the layouts shown overleaf. Before turning the page, you might study them to see how you would have laid out the story—which pictures you would have made large, which small, how arranged and how cropped.

Once again, the real impact of these layouts is lost by their being reproduced so small. To give an idea of the effectiveness of the originals, one picture, given a full page in both LIFE and *Match,* is shown almost original-layout-size on page 92.

How Two Different Designers Laid out the Same Story

Brian Brake's "Monsoon" as It Appeared in LIFE

In the redeeming storm
a cycle of life and death

Brian Brake's "Monsoon" as It Appeared in *Paris-Match*

87

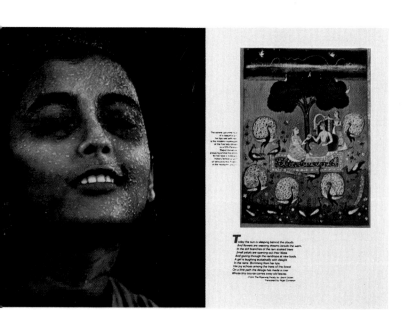

Today the sun is sleeping behind the clouds
And flowers are weaving dreams beside the walls.
In the still branches of the rain-soaked trees
Small petals are opening out their faces.
And gazing through the raindrops at new buds,
A girl is laughing ecstatically with delight.
In the rains. Brimming from her lips
Her joy echoes among the trees of the forest
On a little path the deluge has made a river
Whose tiny course carries away old leaves.
— From The Rhyming Fields by Jibani Guha
Translated by Nigel Cameron

See frolicsome she pours forth her loveliness in a thousand
streams. Her raiment hastily flung around her in dismay
mad passion in her eyes.   Sull of sweetness and joy, she sings.
The anklets on her feet, keeping time, ring out in swift succession,
as if they were sweet cymbals.   The rain has ceased!

and she garbs herself in silken robes embroidered with diamond raindrops
How gay her laughter! How far a dance her smiling footsteps weave!
Her bracelets and bangles circle glittering.   For her earth
and sky swoon away, overflowing with love
— From The Dancer by Anupama Deb

Swing swing Rain Rani, till the flowering of the rose
Swing swing Rain Rani, till the flowering of the mangoit
Swing swing Rain Rani, till the flowering of the champa

Heat dies in the appeasing rain, the woods put out their joy
in yellow flowers, in wind-touched branches, and birds
breaking their copies like bursts of laughter
The season has love garments, for women: robes of mirrors
and jasmine, scarce open-blown flowers
and orange ear rings of the wet kadamba

Dressed in their finest teranous aftir, country women abandon their husbands when swings are put up and a ride Swinging is most in the Stone Garden of the Maharaja's Palace in Udaipur and jaipur. This traditional seasonal women had during the whole year to leave their villages and gather together

le grand festival des balançoires.

Et c'est l'action de grâces
Que la mousson ait été leur salut
sur leur perte, même les vieilles femmes et les
enfants vont au grand rendez-vous du Gange.
Là, ils murmurent les hymnes de
reconnaissance que leur ont appris leurs
ancêtres. Atteignés sont accablés,
ils remercient les dieux de peau de leur
Sans offense et qu'ils ne t'en
vengent l'amour suivante.

Here, uncropped, exactly as they came out of his camera, are 22 pictures from a take of more than 500 shot by Brian Brake for an essay on the monsoon in India. Of the 18 LIFE used and the 17 Paris-Match used, nine were chosen by both.

Pictures That Persuade 3

H. J. PERKINS: *Easy Harvest from Wisconsin Earth*, 1895

The Photographer with a Point of View

Where people and events are concerned, there is no such thing as an objective photograph—any more than there is a truly neutral newspaper. A newspaper editor, by selecting or rejecting a story, by the play he gives it in his paper, even by the choice of the reporter he assigns to cover it, is coloring the news—he cannot help it. Nor can the photographer. For all the widespread belief in the camera as a passionless recorder of events, it, too, colors them because of the man behind the lens; it is his decisions about what to shoot—and when and how—that shape each photograph he takes. Even what seem to be lucky shots of fast-breaking events—toppling buildings, men being murdered—are colored. Each of the stunning news photographs in the first chapter of this volume is colored. Though most are "grab" shots, taken on the run as the event unfolded, they were grabbed in a particular way by men who chose to run in a certain direction, whose reflexes were grooved to certain responses, who had a particular lens or a particular kind of camera. All of these variables, whether chosen consciously or not, were still chosen. And choice inevitably colors.

Coloring is not a dirty word. Nor should a discussion of it have any bearing on the old claim that the "camera cannot lie." Of course it cannot lie—so long as it is accepted that all lenses see differently, and that black-and-white reproduction in two dimensions of three-dimensional colored objects is the "truth." Given these as recognized and acceptable limitations on "truth" in photography, it follows that if there is any lying to be done, it will be done by men and not by instruments. The photographer who sets out to get unusual views of a well-mannered and composed public figure, and who waits and waits for the rare blink, the one yawn, so that he can bring back to the office a set of uncharacteristic, awkward facial expressions, is lying; his camera is not. If in his darkroom he retouches a picture of a woman, removes all her wrinkles, straightens her nose, endows her with cheekbones and a cleavage she does not possess, he is lying. The camera did not.

But if coloring is inevitable—and possible at every step of the photographic process—it can be directed and controlled. The photographer can forget the pejorative implications of the word and make up his mind that his pictures will at least be honestly conceived. It is the very flexibility of photography—the ability to color—that gives him the chance to be an artist, a polemicist or a moralist as he may choose, and also imposes on him a responsibility. For pictures are powerful persuaders; they have been taken for evil purposes in the past and they will be again. As a single example, the official pictures taken of Adolf Hitler were evil because they lied about their subject. They turned a monster into a statesman, making him seem high-minded, modest, patriotic and self-sacrificing.

Condemning a Hitler photograph is easy, but the very fact that pictures are used to persuade brings many of them into a shadowy borderland that makes the passing of a final judgment on them difficult. Consider another example: the charming and surely innocuous composition on page 95. It was taken before the turn of the century and used in a book designed to attract settlers to Wisconsin. It is a most persuasive picture. There stands the farmer, tanned and responsible, surrounded by corn as high as an elephant's eye. What giants those cabbages are, what a bounty of carrots, onions, cucumbers, squashes. What a fine-looking baby. Could any pallid city dweller yearning for a fresh start in a new place ever resist Wisconsin after poring over a picture like this?

But what lies just back of that noble stand of corn, how many bugs, how much drought? How many totally unfit would-be farmers were seduced by this picture into giving up all their savings and all the sweat in their bodies without ever being able to harvest a single squash? On the other hand, how else could Wisconsin have attracted men who *could* make it as farmers?

Hard questions. On examination, coloring opens a Pandora's box of conflicting judgments and priorities. It becomes a force for both good and evil, a molder of thought, a beckoner to opportunity, an instrument for reform, a seller of useless things, a swayer of passions and votes. One man's virtuous persuasion is another man's pernicious propaganda. The concerned photographer, venturing into the world of opinion and events, will quickly find himself making as many moral judgments as esthetic ones. In the end only he can decide what point of view he should express. Of means to convey his idea he has no lack. Almost nothing in photography does not somehow color the result. Even the little matter of emulsion is significant: in the right hands, used the right way, what a powerful persuader emulsion becomes *(pages 98-99)*. Whether for good or evil, a coarse emulsion can help impart a greater sense of menace to a hard-hat workman than can a fine-grain emulsion. Similarly, the choice of artificial or natural light, whether to use color film or black-and-white (not just to show red dresses but for deeper, more persuasive reasons), choice of lens and shutter-speed, darkroom techniques—in fact, everything in photography is a persuader. □

Techniques of Persuasion

Persuasion starts with film itself. The coarseness or fineness of the grain structure of the emulsion can have a strong effect on the mood of a picture. This mood can be intensified by the way the film is developed, and intensified again by the amount the final print is enlarged. All three options are demonstrated by Sebastian Milito in the examples at right. For the near picture Milito used a fast 35mm film with a relatively coarse grain that blurred subtleties of tone and accentuated contrasts of light and dark. For the picture opposite he sought a softer image with a slower film having a finer grain. In addition, Milito shot this picture with 4 x 5 rather than 35mm film, which meant that for reproduction here, the first picture had to be enlarged more than the second, further accentuating its graininess. As a final step, Milito developed the first negative with a high-speed developer to increase its contrast even further, but for the second picture he used a developer that provides normal contrast. The results: one photograph, harsh and belligerent, that gives an immediate impression of dark brooding menace; another with pleasant detail that seems more benign.

This picture was made with a Nikon F, a 50mm (normal) lens and fast film. The coarse grain accentuates the dark shadows under the workman's helmet, out of which peer lowering, menacing eyes. It also makes him look unshaven and calls attention to the hair on his chest and arms. These elements have been further accented by the use of a contrasty, fast developer and by enlargement of the original about seven times the size of the negative.

For a softer result, Milito uses a Burke and James 4 x 5 view camera, a 150mm lens (normal for that camera) and a film only about half as fast as that used for the picture on the opposite page. The enlargement was moderate—twice negative size—retaining middle-gray tones and delicate detail. The immediate impression that this picture gives is far less menacing than that of the one opposite, despite the fact that the pose—with its forward-thrust leg and emphasis on bulging arm muscles—is more aggressive.

Making a Point with Light

Nothing affects the meaning of a picture more than lighting. Here are two pictures made by Yale Joel of the actor-director Howard Da Silva, the one on this page taken indoors with electronic flash, the other outdoors in natural light. The results are extraordinary; one assures us that Da Silva is a troubled man who has seen much of life, the other that he is a benign old gentleman. Flash, with its hard, single-source quality, produces a picture of dramatic contrast: strong shadows and highlights that emphasize Da Silva's wrinkles and the texture of his skin. Its mood is one of remoteness and sadness. The vicissitudes of the years are stamped on this craggy face, whose eyes—dark pupils in the surrounding glare—stare past the camera deep into their owner's private and somber world.

In natural light Da Silva emerges as an entirely different person. He has lived longer—his hair and eyebrows are white, not dark—but his life has been easier. His face is not ravaged, the lines have been largely smoothed away. He gazes serenely at the camera, and helps the illusion of serenity with a gentle smile—a man comfortably at peace with the world.

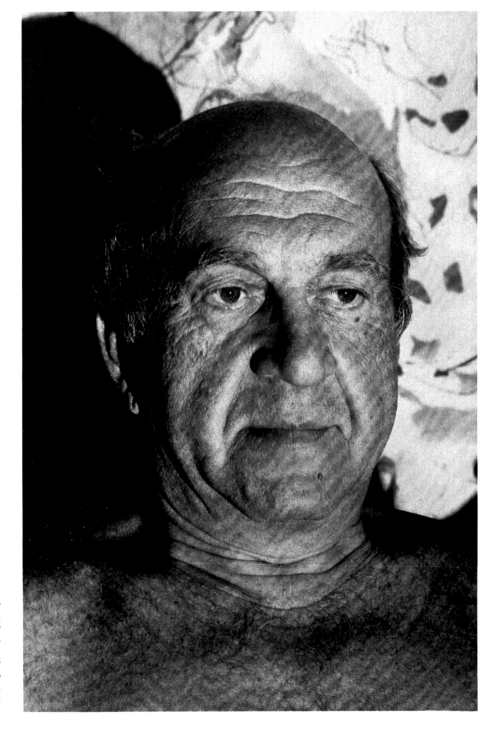

Using a Nikon F and an 85mm lens, Yale Joel strengthened the effect he was after with his strobe unit by keeping it low—at the eye level of the subject. Such a low-angled light source creates unfamiliar shadows for viewers accustomed to looking at faces in light that comes from overhead. Here Da Silva appears to be gazing into the flickering light of a fire, an illusion that is enhanced by the shadow of his head rising up on the wall behind him.

Outdoors, with the same camera and lens, Joel chose the more diffuse natural light of midafternoon for a shot of an easygoing Da Silva. He also lowered his camera position—to about the level of Da Silva's Adam's apple. This change in angle accentuates the effect Joel wanted. Mouth and jaw become more prominent, and Da Silva now can look downward slightly to give his gaze its amiable quality.

Color: Yes or No

Color is so weighted with meaning that even slight alterations—attained by the use of filters or by deliberately overexposing or underexposing—can change the point of a picture. But before the photographer manipulates color he has a more profound editorial decision to make: whether or not to use color at all. In this pair of pictures—a street scene on New York's Lower East Side—a black-and-white shot brings out the squalor of the setting and emphasizes the drabness of lives led there. The same street shot in color becomes a lively, almost festive place. Freelance Marcia Keegan made both pictures on assignment for this book to emphasize just this point. Her own feeling is that her pictures persuade too much—the black-and-white is too drab; the color shot too gay. The truth, she believes, lies somewhere in between.

Shot with a Nikon F and its normal 50mm lens, Marcia Keegan's black-and-white scene is depressing. What hits the viewer is the dirty street, the littered steps, the decaying buildings, the anonymous people resignedly sitting. The one lively note, the rope-jumping girls, is almost lost in the general tawdriness of the scene.

Color warms up the whole scene instantly. A pillar of deep, rich red glows in the center of the picture, and the buildings take on warm shades of blue and green. The people, no longer apathetic, have sprung to life against that colored background by adding several small flickering notes of color themselves.

Interpreting with Shutter Speed

By changing shutter speed to control the appearance of motion, the photographer can produce widely different interpretations of a single event. In one picture of a Toronto street parade, the Canadian freelance Michael Semak chose to emphasize the personality of a single parader. He set his shutter at 1/125 second and froze one girl as she went by. In another, Semak stretched out his exposure to 1/8 second, producing a blur of animated motion. Thus, he first reminds us that parades are made up of individuals marching, carrying headdresses, getting tired feet. Then he asks us to forget the individuals, take our places on the sidewalk and remember that parades are spectator events.

Using a 200mm lens on his Nikon F to get in close, Michael Semak succeeds in drawing the viewer right into the procession (left). He sees one girl so clearly, learns so much about what her costume is made of, that the viewer himself becomes a parader. With the same lens, but stopped down to f/16 to take a 1/8-second exposure, Semak completely depersonalizes the scene (above). Here he speaks of parades in general—anonymous figures whirling past. The viewer can see right through them, a comment on the transitoriness of all parades.

Exploiting Camera Angle

Robert Walch demonstrates how to alter mood and message by a change in camera angle with a pair of pictures of a young couple he encountered in a New Mexico state park. They were headed west, hoping to make a living as traveling musicians—but with no bookings or experience.

For his first picture Walch stood on a picnic table and shot downward, telling the young people's entire story by placing them in a setting that quickly reveals the fragility of their dream. They are gentle innocents, posed hopefully with their guitars and their small stock of other worldly goods in front of the minibus that is their home. The emphasis here is on people, the why and how of their lives.

On the opposite page the emphasis is all on music. With a low camera angle the huge shapes of the guitars become the dominant picture elements. The players have become one with their instruments, their faces romanticized in a setting of soaring trees. Now we are not so much interested in who they are as in what their music is like. We no longer wonder whether they will be able to make it as performers; they *are* performers—their expressions and the picture tell us so.

Walch shot this picture with a Leica M3 and a 35mm wide-angle lens. This lens allowed him to keep fairly close to his subjects and still get them and their bus within his picture frame. The wide angle further strengthens the effect that Walch was seeking by making the bus appear to be small in comparison to its owners.

Using the same 35mm lens, Walch this time makes a horizontal shot, moving in at a low angle until the two guitars spread completely across his picture frame. The emphasis on music—on performance—is intensified by the way in which the wide-angle lens succeeds in bringing up the size of the players' hands.

The Right Lens

Once again, change a single variable and the point of the picture changes. Here there has been a lens change —nothing else. The event was a dinner honoring former Democratic mayors of Westbrook, Maine. As the meal broke up, freelance Tim Kantor took two pictures at a distance of six feet from the evening's principal speaker, Maine's Senator Edmund S. Muskie. In his first picture Kantor wanted to emphasize the political flavor of the evening, so he selected an extreme-wide-angle lens. Depth of field for such a lens is remarkable. Kantor was only a foot or so from the two people coming up to shake their Senator's hand, but they are nonetheless recognizably clear figures, although the focus is on Muskie. Also in focus are the patriotic bunting, the clock and the bingo board in the background. This is the basement of a small-town church, identifiable as such—a place where politicians have wooed voters time and again in rural America.

To make his second picture Kantor switched to a 105mm lens. Instantly the setting disappears; neither a political meeting nor a popular politician exists. What little background remains is a blur, and Kantor has produced a picture of a man—a pleasant-looking man, granted, but not necessarily a senator out working to win votes.

Tim Kantor used a Nikon F and a 24mm lens to give him the extreme depth of field he needed to keep both Senator Muskie and a pair of admirers in relatively sharp focus in this picture. Kantor elected to stand only six feet away from Muskie; if he had been much farther away the wide angle of his lens would have made the Senator appear too small.

Still standing six feet from his subject, but switching to a 105mm lens, Kantor fills his frame with Muskie's face for a close-up of the Senator. The shallow depth of field provided by this lens blurs everything else, and thus concentrates on the Senator's personality rather than on the political flavor of the evening.

Changing Emphasis by Changing Camera Position

Another public gathering in another church, this time in the First Methodist Church of Keyser, West Virginia, where the Women's Club has invited Prosecuting Attorney Byron Athey to speak to its members on the drug problem. Instead of remaining in one spot and simply changing lenses, as was done in a similar situation on pages 108-109, the photographer, William Kuykendall, did something quite different. He used the same lens for each of three pictures, but moved around in the room, altering his composition in such a way that he obtained three pictures that make three entirely different points.

For his first picture Kuykendall took up a position at the back of the room. By strongly emphasizing the heads of the audience, he has driven home the point that this is a crowded meeting, and that those present are listening with close attention to the speaker.

For his second picture, Kuykendall moved around to the side of the room. The point of emphasis is no longer people but empty chairs. With this change, the speaker, instead of being a man easily holding a large audience, becomes one who has trouble holding a small one.

For this third exposure, Kuykendall moved close. Now all the camera sees is the speaker and the lectern with its cross. Presto! A Prosecuting Attorney transformed into a lay preacher—who may or may not have an attentive congregation. All three shots were made with a 35mm lens on a Nikon F.

Doctoring in the Darkroom

Much can be done in the darkroom to make a persuasive picture out of a negative that has its obvious virtues but equally obvious drawbacks. Joel Snyder demonstrates with a picture he took of rock singer Janis Joplin in her dressing room not long before her death in 1970. Struck by the extremely theatrical way she used her hands even when she was not onstage, Snyder snapped her in the act of asking her manager for a cup of tea. Under the harsh light of a single overhead bulb, he obtained a negative that, printed without any dark-room manipulation *(above),* presents a picture of an awkwardly gesticulating woman, not particularly attractive. But that was not what Miss Joplin was; by work in the darkroom, Snyder came closer to the truth, or what he perceived the truth to be *(shown opposite).*

A print made from Snyder's original catch-as-catch-can shot (opposite) reveals an awkward door in one corner of the picture, and a deadly white background. It also gives Miss Joplin a very rough complexion. Snyder got rid of these drawbacks, and at the same time created a dramatic "onstage" picture by print manipulation (above). His first step in the darkroom was to soften Miss Joplin's complexion by putting a double thickness of nylon stocking over his enlarger lens to diffuse the image it projected. He then burned in and darkened the objectionable background of his print by lengthening the exposure, meanwhile holding his hand over the center so that the image of Miss Joplin's face would not be affected. As a result she is framed in brightness —an artificial spotlight that puts her onstage.

Manipulating the Truth by Cropping

Cropping can greatly strengthen a photograph by focusing attention on its main point through the elimination of distracting, ugly or irrelevant details. Such changes, while usually made for esthetic reasons, can also be used to alter completely the meaning of the pic-ture, and even to perpetrate a fraud. Never has cropping been misused quite so brazenly as it was in 1954, when the late Senator Joseph McCarthy attempt-ed to discredit Secretary of the Army Robert Stevens with the picture above, cropped as shown opposite.

This is the full print of a snapshot made of Army Secretary Stevens standing with Private G. David Schine, a former McCarthy aide, and two other men. McCarthy, trying to make it seem that Stevens was attempting to be friendly with Schine, had the other men cropped out.

Cropped as shown at right, it now does appear that Stevens is solicitous of Schine and eager to be seen with him. Luckily Stevens' counsel Joseph Welch got hold of the original picture and was able to expose the fraud—which ultimately helped destroy the Senator.

Finding the Telling Moment

Nobody can teach the photographer when to trip his shutter. This he must learn by himself through long practice and through the recollection of many missed opportunities—fortified by an instinctive ability to sense the emotional peak of an event. It is often possible to recognize ahead of time something special about the subject and then concentrate on capturing that special quality—a gesture, a shadow across a face, the glow of late light, a pile of wreckage. Above all else, the photographer should learn to wait. The decisive moment may not be the actual crash of two cars, but later, when a child stares at a dead body in the street. Professionals keep shooting as they wait; film is cheap and they never know if a better shot than the one just made will come.

The contact sheet at right is a fine example of a subject understood and patience rewarded. It shows 25 frames from a roll of film taken by LIFE photographer Alfred Eisenstaedt of Winston Churchill at a political rally. Eisenstaedt did the best he could as the meeting dragged on, but Churchill was obviously bored and sat there looking cold and grumpy. Then, Eisenstaedt says: "The band started to play 'God Save the King.' Instantly he shot up, wide awake, making his famous V-for-victory sign like an automatic action. Frame 25 was the telling picture." ☐

Eisenstaedt's contact sheet records one unproductive shot after another of an obviously bored Winston Churchill—frame 24 shows him beginning to drowse. The roll of film was almost used up before Eisenstaedt's patience and alertness paid off—the rally picked up, Churchill made a characteristic gesture and Eisenstaedt obtained a shot his magazine could use.

*Here is a blowup of the successful frame 25.
...nce Eisenstaedt was not allowed to approach
...close, he chose a 90mm lens to fill the picture
frame of his Leica, and came up with a fine
...ews shot of a rugged old campaigner making
the celebrated gesture that was his hallmark.*

ALFRED EISENSTAEDT: *Churchill,* 1951

The Passionate Camera

In room 235 of the Library of Congress, a hushed and high-ceilinged chamber, there is a collection of nearly 150,000 photographs. Edward Steichen, himself one of the century's master photographers, calls the pictures in this collection "the most remarkable human documents ever rendered in pictures." The photographs are unglamorous, unflattering, even unattractive. Their subjects are as simple as the woman's work-gnarled hands shown on the opposite page. But all of the photographs are eloquent without being repellent; because in all of them can be seen the compassionate—and often passionate—understanding of the photographer. The collection has become famous as a classic example of how a photojournalist's pictures can persuade: they are, as another critic labeled them, "pictures that altered America." The pictures were taken during the Depression in the 1930s, by photographers of the Farm Security Administration.

Photographers in the *Farm Security Administration?* This is how they got there and what they did.

In the early 1930s, as America's worst Depression spread across the country, the farmers were the most gravely hurt. Farm prices already had been plummeting, and mechanization had been driving the small farmer from his land or into tenancy. Then the worst drought and series of dust storms in history almost denuded the American plains. In April of 1935 President Franklin D. Roosevelt created the Resettlement Administration, later to be renamed the Farm Security Administration, to help relocate the dispossessed farmer. To head the project Roosevelt chose Columbia University Economist Rexford Guy Tug-

well. And Tugwell, quite aware of the controversy such a massive resettlement project would arouse in a conservative Congress, sent for a Columbia colleague to help persuade the public of the need for federal help.

His colleague seemed an unlikely one for the job. Roy Stryker was an engineer and an economist. But he also had a flair for illustration. And he decided that the persuasive tool he would use was the photograph—"the photograph," he said, "that little rectangle, that's one of the damnedest educational devices that was ever made." Roy Stryker was no photographer—"I wouldn't know how to take a photograph of my aunt," he said—but with the assurance of a nonphotographer, he set out to persuade the people with the help of men and women who already were photographers or would quickly learn to be photographers.

Many of them have become legendary by now: Walker Evans, Dorothea Lange, Carl Mydans, Arthur Rothstein, Marion Post Wolcott, Russell Lee, John Vachon, and even Ben Shahn, who took some of the best photographs but later returned to his painting. Their photographs swept the country, in newspapers, magazines and exhibitions. And they persuaded as perhaps no other collection of photographs ever has: all of urban America was made poignantly and painfully aware of a serious imbalance in United States society. Returning prosperity finally absorbed the dispossessed and somewhat alleviated their agony. But not before Roy Stryker had proved that a small but passionate army of photographers can make a historic contribution to the development of photojournalism.

Her leathery hands, gnarled from working the harsh land of an Iowa homestead, are all this farm woman has to show for her efforts. When photographer Russell Lee found her, the family was on relief, and Lee realized that the woman's hands alone told her whole story.

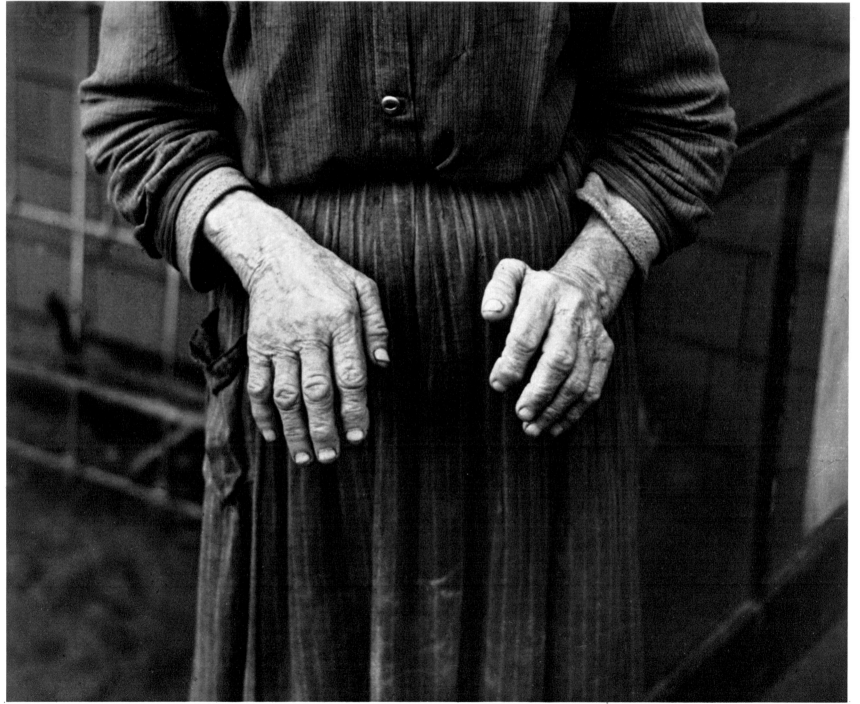

RUSSELL LEE: *Iowa Homesteader's Wife,* 1936

Faces of Defeat

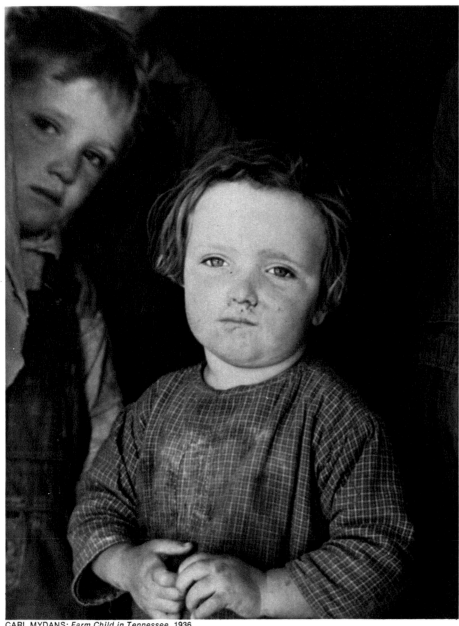

CARL MYDANS: *Farm Child in Tennessee*, 1936

*The hollow eyes and smudged face of poverty
are portrayed in Carl Mydans' picture of a child
he found on the Natchez Trace, on a federal
works project near Lexington, Tennessee.*

It was the haunting look of defeat —more than the tattered tents, the ragged clothes and the bony limbs —that made the most lasting impression on the FSA photographers. And through their close-up pictures of these eloquent faces they tried to convey to the rest of America a sense of the long dull pain of hunger and want.

Back they would come to Washington, where with quiet voice and withering eye Roy Stryker would ask, "Why did you shoot this? What are you trying to say?" Carl Mydans recalls him asking, "Why in the hell did that so-and-so stand here? Don't tell me because there was a fence or a tree in front of him. All I care about is whether or not it's a good picture." Under Stryker's soft-voiced but ceaseless questioning, prodding, hectoring and lecturing, his photographers learned how to convert an emotionless face into an emotional persuasion, how to make a ravaged cornfield into a message for mankind.

Some of Stryker's students even had to learn the fundamentals of photography. Stryker handed a Leica to artist Ben Shahn and said, "Go out and fool around with it." Shahn came back with some photographs that were simply awful, and others *(right)* that glowed with compassion. Stryker waved the best ones at the other photographers and cried, "Look what Shahn has done, and he doesn't know one part of a camera from another." Thus challenged, the others went out and tried, in the words of one of the best, Dorothea Lange, to "say something about the despised, the defeated, the alienated. . . . About the crippled, the helpless, the rootless. . . . About duress and trouble. . . . About the last ditch."

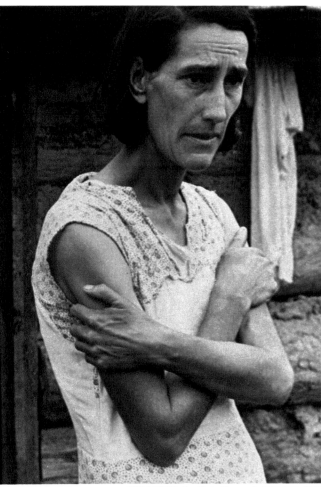

BEN SHAHN: *Destitute Woman in Arkansas, 1935*

What he lacked in experience as a photographer, artist Ben Shahn made up for with compassion as he recorded the gaunt despair on the face of this Arkansas woman (above) whose family had been dispossessed from the farm that had been their livelihood.

DOROTHEA LANGE: *Old Man, California, 1936*

Little better off than the migrants, the field bosses frequently sympathized with the newcomers. This labor contractor in California, called "One-Eye Charlie," told photographer Lange, "I'm making my living off of these people, so I know the conditions."

121

Studies in Determination and Despair

JOHN VACHON: *Ozark Mountain Family,* 1940

The dogged determination with which some families clung to their land impressed photographer John Vachon, who portrayed this Ozark family standing straight and stubborn on the porch of their shabby cabin. Many an Ozark farmer stuck it out through the Depression.

In contrast to the determined holdouts above, ▶ Dorothea Lange found in California a family (opposite) who had made the difficult decision to try to find a better land. They had left Oklahoma and made the trek to California, only to find a hopeless existence in a makeshift tent.

DOROTHEA LANGE: *Okie Family,* 1936

A Spirit Tested by Poverty and Nature

WALKER EVANS: *Cabin In Alabama, 1935*

A classic study in simplicity was achieved by Walker Evans' photograph of a tenant farmer's cabin in Alabama. The patterned oilcloth, the clean threadbare towel, the wooden cupboard at the rear of the room, the washbowl on the shelf in the foreground, even the texture of the clean-washed wooden walls—all affirmed the spirit of a people impoverished but still proud. Walker Evans was one of the few FSA photographers who was able to teach Stryker himself. Says Stryker: "I saw his pictures, I walked at night with him and I talked to him. He told me about what the photographer was for, what a photographer should do. . . . I was caught between my own selfish rationalization of the project and the photographers' unselfish rationalization, and I profited by both sides."

One of the most famous photographs to come ▶ out of the FSA program was this picture of the onset of a dust storm. Months of drought had turned great areas of the Midwest into a dust bowl, and farmers who had somehow survived the market decline were now confronted with natural disaster as all their topsoil was blown away. On a farm in Cimarron County, Oklahoma, FSA photographer Arthur Rothstein caught the poignant moment in a dust storm as a father and two sons raced for shelter, one of the boys shielding his eyes from the flying soil. The half-buried stumps, the dune-mounded outbuilding and the wasteland surrounding the retreating people added to the impact of a memorable photograph that came to stand for "dust bowl" more than any other evidence of the era.

ARTHUR ROTHSTEIN: *Dust Storm in Oklahoma,* 1936

"What We Do Want Is a Chanst..."

DOROTHEA LANGE: *Headed West, Texas, 1937*

As dispossessions and dust storms drove them out, the farmers headed west, and the FSA photographers followed them. One who caught the mood of the immigration was Dorothea Lange, who took the pictures on these and the next six pages. She recalled the brave, bitter words of these nomads: "We hold ourselves to be decent folks. We don't want no relief. But what we do want is a chanst to make an honest living like what we was raised."

With only a carriage and wheelbarrow for transportation, a family heads west in Dorothea Lange's photograph. They left Arkansas for the Rio Grande Valley, to pick cotton.

Nearing the end of their journey, two families ▶ stop their overburdened cars to check the route. They often traveled muddy back roads because their licenses had expired.

DOROTHEA LANGE: *Cars Going West,* 1936

Disillusion in the Promised Land

DOROTHEA LANGE: *Shaving on the Road, California, 1937*

Still concerned about his appearance, but unconcerned by the presence of photographer Lange, a migrant sits by the road and shaves with a makeshift mirror attached to the side of his car before setting out early to find work as a potato picker. To get a job he had to be in town early, when the labor contractors rounded up their crews for the day's work in the fields.

After the long hegira, the newcomers to California found themselves in tent settlements worse than the dust-blasted farmhouses they had left. Traveling among these encampments photographer Lange found scenes like this where the children sat amidst the refuse while both their parents were out working in the fields.

DOROTHEA LANGE: *Okie Homes in California*, 1936

The Apathy of the Unwanted

DOROTHEA LANGE: *Old Men, California*, 1937

The apathy and resignation of three Depression victims, sitting in the dust of a California town and waiting for their relief checks, is recorded by Dorothea Lange's camera. Roy Stryker later praised "the great feeling for human beings she had. This never failed to show in her work."

The daughter of a migrant from Tennessee ▶ despondently waits out the long day in the family tent home in the American River Camp near Sacramento. Photographer Lange quoted another such migrant as saying: "I've wrote back that we're well and such as that, but I never have wrote that we live in a tent."

DOROTHEA LANGE: *Migrant Girl*, 1936

Portrait of a Modern Peasantry

In one summer during her career with the FSA, Dorothea Lange put 17,000 miles on her speedometer. She was touring the South, where she found the most impoverished and desperate victims of the Depression: the blacks.

The Negro sharecropper in the U.S. South during the 1930s worked to exhaustion—"from can to can't," as he put it. He averaged barely 65 cents a day for the labor of his entire family, and he rarely saw any of the money anyway since he could never get ahead of the debt he owed for the "furnish," the advance of food and clothing made to him, often at above-market prices, by the landowner. So entangled in debt was the black sharecropper that he could not even escape to the West like his white counterpart. As the fatalistic black rhyme put it, "A jot's a jot; a figger's a figger. All for the white man, and none for the nigger."

Tramping through the Alabama farmland, photographer Lange found one family that seemed as reminiscent of peasants of the old world as of the new. And her evocative portrait of this family *(right)* called attention to the most oppressed Americans of them all.

In a picture which has become a classic, Dorothea Lange photographed this black family of Alabama sharecroppers at work in the field. Her composition resembles a Millet painting of 19th Century peasants.

DOROTHEA LANGE: *Sharecroppers in Alabama,* 1936

The Other Americans

While thousands of the dispossessed struggled or starved and millions of other Americans suffered through the Depression, a tiny fraction of the population continued to enjoy their luxuries. Roy Stryker was fascinated by the striking contrast between the millionaires and the migrants, and sent one of his FSA photographers, Marion Post Wolcott, down to Miami Beach, Florida, where the Roney Plaza charged as much as $75 a night and a Beach & Tennis Club membership cost $2,300. Photographer Wolcott came back with a portfolio of pictures that added their powerful part to the persuasion that indeed something was greatly out of balance in the America of the 1930s. ☐

Framed and dwarfed by the vaulted entrance to a Miami Beach hotel, an impeccable vacationer steps out for a walk. Photographer Marion Wolcott also caught the moment as an ordinary passerby surveyed the cavernous entrance, staircase and lobby with understandable awe.

MARION POST WOLCOTT: *Entrance to Miami Beach Hotel*, 1939

Photojournalism for Amateurs

Making Personal Pictures Tell a Story 138

EVELYN HOFER: *Tools for a Picture Story*, 1970

Making Personal Pictures Tell a Story

The techniques developed by professional photojournalists—particularly those used in the creation of the picture essay *(pages 51-92)*—turn out to work surprisingly well for the amateur photographer. They not only make shooting pictures more interesting, but also make the results more useful and enjoyable—to everyone who sees them. Many amateurs' albums are a deadly bore, containing every picture ever taken, printed all the same size and pasted down in the order in which they were taken. But albums don't have to be so dull. The pages can resemble those of a magazine layout, suitably organized in varying depths and widths to tell a story whose meaning will be apparent to a viewer at a glance. And slide shows, too, can be transformed into fascinating entertainment by applying the photojournalist's techniques of planning, editing and organizing; the result will be a coherent narrative, in effect a movie made up of still pictures.

The essence of those techniques lies in the word "story"—yet the story does not have to be of world-shaking importance. The amateur cannot record voyages to the moon, but he can convert a drawerful of old snapshots into a touching account of a family member's life, and he can elevate the usual humdrum snapshots of a historic site into an impressionistic recollection of a past long gone.

To do so, however, he must do what the professionals do: plan out the essay he wants to produce. This can be done even if the story must be created from an existing collection of old pictures, but it is easier to plan in advance, looking ahead to photographs that will be needed to tell the story and then going out to shoot them. Not that the pictures for a photo essay are posed; they are, rather, anticipated.

Professional photographers come armed to an assignment with a shooting script, prepared by editors after considerable research into the story idea and consultation with the photographer. Such scripts may be detailed and elaborate. Consider a hypothetical picture story: one on a fire company. The script might call for several different kinds of pictures: major shots that will establish the framework of the narrative (views of the firehouse and close-ups of individual firemen working on the engines), transitional pictures that can be used to guide the viewer from one idea to another (the hook-and-ladder tearing out of the firehouse en route to an alarm), action pictures that convey the drama of fire fighting (the burning building, a fireman overcome by smoke), pictures that bring the story to a conclusion (the exhausted firemen drinking coffee back in the firehouse).

The amateur's shooting script need not be so detailed. To prepare a picture essay on the Cub Scouts' visit to the zoo, for example, he might jot down in advance the few shots he considers essential to his narrative—the Scouts boarding the bus, the stop for lunch. And, like the professional, he must remain flexible as the action unfolds, taking additional pictures that his script may not call for. Although he is not in search of a single great picture, he may find one, and if he is alert he will not fail to get the shot of the tearful boy who drops his ice-cream cone. But the script is necessary because it keeps the photographer on the track, guaranteeing a story with a beginning, a middle and an end—a series of related photographs that becomes a single, storytelling entity.

In search of this goal, the professional does not scrimp on film. Neither should an amateur, for film is the cheapest part of his equipment. If he holds back, waiting for the perfect shot, he misses the tearful Cub Scout. But there are other reasons to take many pictures. Some inevitably turn out wrongly exposed, out of focus or awkwardly composed. But even if every shot is technically and artistically praiseworthy, a large selection is still necessary. In pictorial storytelling, taking the photographs is only the beginning. The negatives that the photographer brings home are the raw materials for a second creative process: choosing pictures to be used; deciding which are the major ones, which the minor; and arranging them in a layout to communicate the story. At this point, the amateur transforms himself from the photographer on assignment to editor and art director; building his picture story by himself he wears in turn the hats of a number of different professionals.

Basic Tool: The Contact Sheet

Following a shooting script and picking up any additional pictures that promise to be useful, the photographer intent on creating a picture essay brings back a considerable number of shots. From these raw materials—the "take"—the essay must now be painstakingly constructed. The basic tool in this process is what is known as the "contact sheet" or "proof sheet," a positive of negatives printed actual size. The contact sheet shown at right is a composite of several that were used to create the picture essay on pages 142-145. With a magnifying glass and marking crayon, or "grease pencil" *(page 137),* the editor examines his tiny prints, choosing those that make a contribution to the narrative he wishes to present. Then he examines these "saves," deciding which he wants to enlarge to emphasize major points in his story, which to print small for use as transitions linking sections of the story together.

Preliminary cropping can also be done directly on the contact sheet to improve the composition of each selected picture or to eliminate extraneous areas that divert attention from its purpose in the story. By judicious cropping it is possible, for instance, to convert a picture containing several people into one showing a single character in the essay. To visualize how cropping alters a photograph, the unwanted areas can be covered with two pieces of paper cut to form right angles. Then the area to be retained is outlined with the grease pencil.

Now the selected shots can be divided and grouped by a number or letter key to create episodes within the story. Each episode will usually occupy a "spread" of two facing pages, so the viewer can grasp their meaning as a unit. The spreads then become the basic elements that, one after another, carry the narrative to its conclusion.

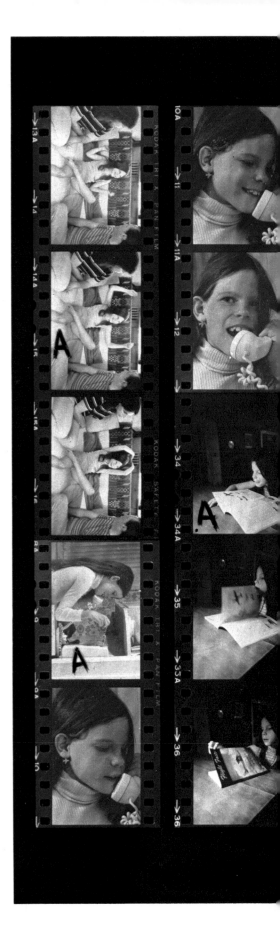

The composite contact sheet shown here was constructed to illustrate how a picture essay could be created from eight rolls of film recording a little girl's first airplane ride. The pictures marked A were used to build the episode for the first spread of facing pages (pages 142-143), those marked B to make up the second spread (pages 144-145).

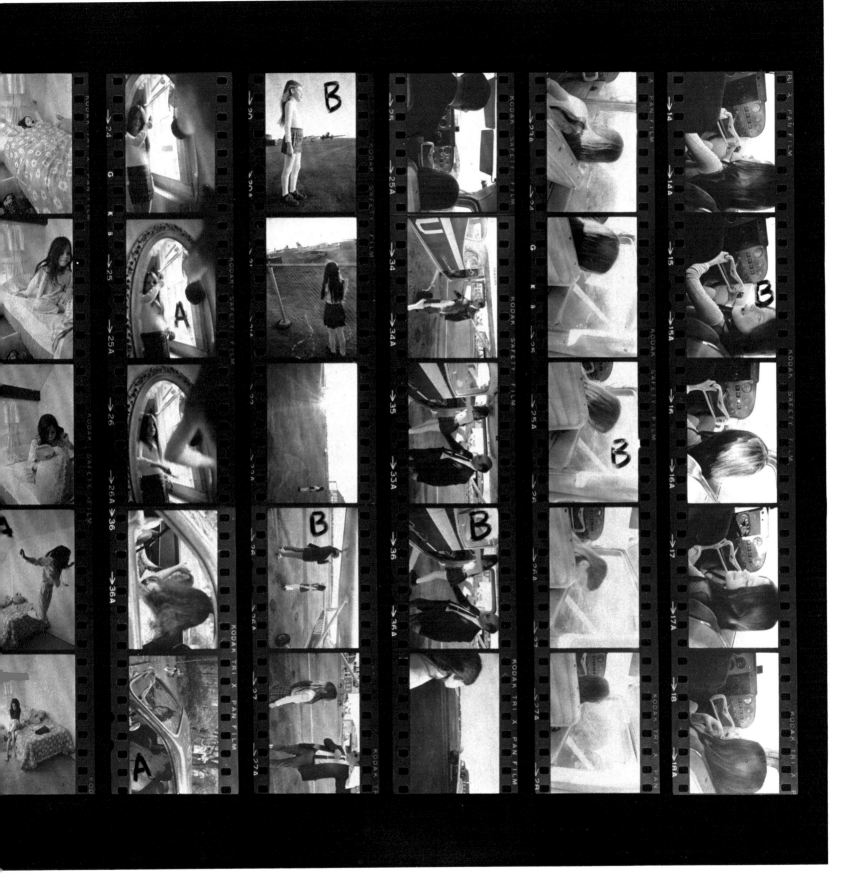

A Day in the Life of Maud Humphrey

*Enlarged from the contacts on the preceding
pages, these pictures form the opening spread
in a kind of picture essay photojournalists
call "a day in the life of. . . ." In this
case photographer Henry Humphrey uses
professional techniques to tell the tale of the 24
hours spanning his nine-year-old daughter
Maud's first airplane ride. The basic idea is
conveyed immediately to the viewer with the
picture above, in which Maud learns the news,
then the plot is swiftly carried forward by the
picture at right, above, in which she excitedly
telephones a friend—a shot that was not in the
photographer's shooting script, but one that
serves as an effective transition between
the opening and the scene of Maud reading up
on airplanes (right) before going to bed.*

As dawn breaks in the Humphrey household, an excited little girl jumps from bed (top, left). The photographer was ready; his shooting script called for this shot and for one like that at left, in which Maud primps in her mirror. Above, the picture essay flows on as Maud and her parents leave for her airplane ride while sisters and friends from the neighborhood look on. This big transition picture brings the spread to a close, completing one episode of the story, and simultaneously invites the viewer to turn the page of the book (or the amateur photographer's album) to see what happens next.

An enlarged picture of Maud dominates the final spread of her picture story (and the airfield and airplane to which she has come). It is frame 20 from the contact sheet on page 141, clearly the one that, setting the locale of the second part of *A Day in the Life of Maud Humphrey*, should be shown large to remind the viewer of the story line. Above, she listens to a few words from the pilot before actually boarding—again, a shot that leads the viewer on in the story.

Maud clambers aboard the plane (above) in a picture that both visually and logically flows out of the photograph to its left. The story line thus continues pictorially; aloft at right above she searches for her home; at right she is permitted to pretend that she has assumed control of the plane. She has yet to land, but the high point of *A Day in the Life of Maud Humphrey* has been reached, and there her essay fittingly ends.

Reproducing the Flavor of a Historic Site

The pictures brought home from most trips are all too familiar: Mother and children posed on the steps of the Lincoln Memorial, the view from the hotel window, the White House from outside the gate—pleasant to have as souvenirs, but essentially meaningless except to the photographer and his family. A picture essay with an imaginative story line can, however, give character and meaning to the scenes brought back from trips.

The pictures on this and the following pages show what can be done if picture taking is planned in advance. The destination of the trip was Mystic Seaport, a restored 19th Century whaling village in Connecticut, and the intent was to re-create history, to show the town as it might really have looked a century ago. Ordinarily, however,

Mystic is jammed with people; it is not only a popular tourist attraction but a favorite port of call for cruising pleasure boats. The photographer, Evelyn Hofer, solved the problem in two ways: by arising early to take some of her pictures before anyone else was abroad and by concentrating on details in other pictures, from which people are necessarily excluded.

The picture essay begins with a scene-setting spread: a big overall view of Seaport Street that includes the full-rigged ship *Joseph Conrad* and the little shops huddled along the cobblestone street by the waterfront. With no people in contemporary clothing in sight, the mood is established: the years are rolled back, and the viewer is invited to take a tour of the old seaport as it appeared in the 19th Century.

From the beckoning sweep of the opening picture on the preceding spread, the camera moves in as the Mystic essay develops. At top the photographer has caught the quiet pace of old Mystic—and two aspects of its life—in a view of a narrow street with Fishtown Chapel in the background and the tavern to the right. Below is a detail of the front porch of a private residence, in which only an air conditioner intrudes into the 20th Century. Opposite, the viewer is brought still closer, seeing another detail of a flower-hung porch, an invitation to come inside the house—and, again, to turn the page to the next spread of the album.

The camera moves closer and closer, taki[n]
viewer further into 19th Century Mystic, loc[k]
at left into the parlor of Thomas Greenman[,]
prominent shipbuilder. Here, the initial pro[blem]
faced by the photographer solves itself;
anachronistic tourists cannot intrude beca[use]
they are not allowed to enter certain areas[,]
restored rooms such as these. The absenc[e of]
people makes the illusion complete, and
re-emphasizes the story line; behind the v[iewer,]
it might be imagined, stand the shipbuilde[r and]
his lady, bringing tea. Below, the printer of [the]
Mystic Press seems to have just stepped o[ut;]
might return in a moment to take an ad
announcing next week's seamen's benefit.

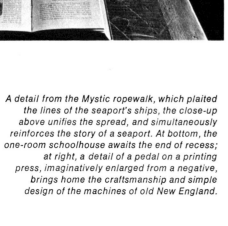

A detail from the Mystic ropewalk, which plaited the lines of the seaport's ships, the close-up above unifies the spread, and simultaneously reinforces the story of a seaport. At bottom, the one-room schoolhouse awaits the end of recess; at right, a detail of a pedal on a printing press, imaginatively enlarged from a negative, brings home the craftsmanship and simple design of the machines of old New England.

The Story behind the Story

Behind every story that might be made into a picture essay lies another—less obvious but often considerably more interesting. One of the most common essays constructed by photographers tells the story of a wedding: the bride poses with her bridesmaids, enters the church with her father . . . and, after the reception, drives off to the honeymoon with her groom. There is nothing wrong with such an essay; it can be handled with the same "day-in-the-life-of" treatment given Maud Humphrey and her airplane ride on pages 142-145. But the story can take on added dimen-

sions if the photographer treats it with the photojournalistic technique known as "telling the story behind the story." This essay, shot by Sebastian Milito, does not begin on the wedding day but a week earlier, when the young couple obtains the license *(above, left).* This small photograph is an indication that larger things are to come: the shopping for the trousseau, the preparation of the apartment into which the newlyweds will move, the alterations to the wedding gown, and the church rehearsal —another transition picture that pulls the viewer toward the next spread.

152

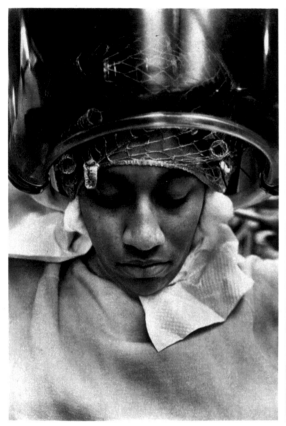

This layout of pictures functions like an arrow, rushing the viewer to the climax of the story. The bride-to-be visits the hairdresser, applies makeup on the wedding morning as her maid-of-honor watches, and prepares to put on her veil before leaving for the ceremony. All these pictures are obviously subordinate to the high point of the story behind the story. That's the radiant bride, at right, opposite, waiting in the church for her attendants to assemble. In size and position, this photograph is climactic; the story behind the story ends at the very moment when most wedding picture stories begin.

Picture stories do not have to be shot from scratch. Some of the best are created by selecting photographs from existing sources. Professionals create such "pickup" essays by searching out the best relevant pictures in photographers' files ("The Passionate Camera" on pages 118-134 was picked up from pictures taken by photographers of the United States Farm Security Administration). The amateur has equally rich sources much closer to hand—family albums *(left and opposite)* and boxes of pictures gathering dust in the attic. Disorganized, unsorted, pasted—good and bad alike—into the albums just in the order the rolls were taken and the local drugstore printed them, they tell no story. Yet from such a mishmash, a judicious selection laid out to a predetermined story line can become an evocative essay on a family's past.

The pickup essay on the following pages—the story of the life of a New York woman—was constructed from cluttered family-album pages like the four shown here. The pictures checked are those selected for the essay—each one clearly showed the principal character in the story and marked a significant point in her life.

A Life Retraced in Old Photographs

Mother's birthplace, 1887

Mother at 3, with friend

Her brood increases

Fourth-grade chums, 1896

A young lady of 11

Easter finery, 1893

Kate Louise Knapp Vondermuhll was a girl from a prominent New York family. Born in 1887, she grew up in the city, summered in Connecticut, married, traveled, became the mother of three children and the grandmother of five before her death in 1955. Here and on the pages overleaf, the story of that life emerges as layout and design focus on pictures drawn from several Knapp-Vondermuhll albums. The variations in picture sizes were introduced partly by picture selection—some of the photographs were snapshots, others professional cabinet prints—and partly by cropping with scissors. Arrangement of these on the spreads then transformed Mrs. Vondermuhll from an anonymous figure lost amid an album hodgepodge; she became an individual seen in the era in which she lived.

Primping at the Litchfield Club

Picking posies on the Palisades

Pa Richards

Mother and a beau, about 1903

Seventeenth Summer

Mother dressed for a Sunday call, 1908

Wedding day, November 11, 1911

Father and Mother, and George Jr. makes three, 1912

And Kitty makes four, 1915

In our new home on 79th Street

nice, 1926: The Grand Tour

Our first plane ride, Basel

Those chic long dresses, 1934

The first grandchild, 1938

The Many Uses of Pictures in Sequence

The basic technique of the picture essay—presenting a number of related events in a meaningful sequence of photographs—turns out to be very useful in ways that seem remote from the essay form. A set of pictures in chronological sequence, for example, can record the building of a neighbor's house, perhaps to make a gift album. Or step-by-step procedures can be made clear in pictures—a "how-to" sequence outlining the cooking of a favorite dish might be used in the photographer's own household or serve as a gift, perhaps for a daughter-in-law.

For a cooking sequence like the one at left, the procedures developed by TIME-LIFE BOOKS' Foods of the World series call for a detailed script. If a dish has been made many times, it is easy for the cook to forget to mention an essential step. The photographer should keep shooting; a missed action usually means that the entire dish has to be recooked. Editing such a sequence also requires special care.

Color is a real advantage in cooking how-to's, and it also serves a useful purpose in a house-construction sequence like that at right, originally shot for LIFE. The transition from bare and scrubby lot to house with landscaped grounds becomes impressive.

A pictorial recipe for authentic Boston baked beans: (1) Cover two pounds of beans with water; soak overnight; the skins should burst when blown on. (2) Press a whole peeled onion into the beans until it is just covered. (3) Score a piece of salt pork, spread it and lay it on top. (4) Pour a mixture of ¾ cup molasses, ¾ cup brown sugar, 1 tablespoon salt, 1 teaspoon pepper and 1 tablespoon dry mustard over the dish. Add enough boiling water to cover the contents of the pot, cover and bake at 250° to 300° for at least nine hours. (5) Remove the cover and bake another hour to crisp the pork.

A prefabricated house springs from an empty lot on Block Island, Rhode Island, as the camera catches a flatbed truck bearing materials to the site (1), pictures the house four days after the start of construction in a side view (2) and a front view (3) and finally presents the building ready for occupancy eight weeks later (4).

Essay on a Wall

The great photographer Edward Steichen pioneered in more than one area of the art. In a series of exhibits of his own pictures over the years, he revolutionized the showing of photographs, scaling and placing them, in the words of René d'Harnoncourt, the late director of the Museum of Modern Art in New York, "to create a collective image or a sequence of images to convey the overall content of the exhibition in a dramatic manner." In effect, employing the sequential technique seen on pages 162-163, Steichen made the walls of museums into large-scale picture es-says—a professional photojournalistic method that can be put to use on a living-room wall, or on the bulletin boards of the local school or library.

The example of an essay on a wall shown on these pages uses four of the several hundred photographs Steichen took of a shad-blow tree in his backyard in West Redding, Connecticut, over a period of years. "I tried to weave them into a consecutive series, thinking of it as a concerto," Steichen once said, "with the little tree the solo instrument and the neighboring trees and pond the members of the orchestra."

The sequence of the seasons marches across the spread in this Steichen series. In summer (opposite, left) his little shad-blow tree near the center of the scene is almost obscured by other foliage. In fall (opposite, right) it joins its neighbors in an outburst of autumn color; then in winter (above, left) it stands alone. Finally, in spring, Steichen's story ends as the tree once again bursts forth in bloom for another year.

Slides for a Hit Show

An invitation to "come over and see the slides we took on our trip" is generally looked forward to about as much as a visit to the dentist. Yet a slide show can be entertaining for any audience—family, friends or strangers—if it is produced the way a photojournalist produces a picture essay. The best shows come from pictures that are at least partly planned in advance, so narrative elements are provided, arranged in a sequence and finally edited—ruthlessly edited—to eliminate substandard pictures and to keep the show short.

These principles were followed in producing a show from the slides at right and overleaf. It tells a routine story—one family's summer vacation on the Massachusetts island of Martha's Vineyard—but it tells a complete story, logically organized.

From the opening slide, a chart of the Vineyard marked to show the vacation house and places that will be visited, the story moves swiftly forward. The cast—freelance photographer Don Hinkle, his wife Penny and their children Kathy and Debbie—is introduced. Then a signpost indicates that the family is going on a trip. Such important transition shots are preplanned.

But, while following his script, Hinkle did not overlook events that might contribute spontaneity; illness and a rainy day *(overleaf)* can make up a substory.

For the 24-slide story on these pages, photographer Hinkle shot more than 50 rolls of film—perhaps more than an amateur might wish to expend over a summer. But it is only by shooting generously that the "take" for the story provides enough pictures to create a narrative—and enough to throw away that do not help the narrative.

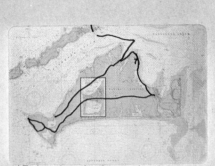

1 | *To introduce the show, a chart locates the vacation scene on Martha's Vineyard: East Chop, Gay Head, Oak Bluffs, Menemsha Bight, Vineyard Haven.*

2 | *The quartet of vacationers and their summer home in East Chop: Don and Penny below on the porch, Kathy and Debbie perched above on the roof.*

6 | *...but both of them did manage to learn to swim that summer back at the calmer beach at East Chop.*

7 | *Off on a tour of the island—as this pre-planned signpost shot heralds—the family heads into the village of Oak Bluffs...*

11 | *Afterward, there was a pause to have a look at a swan nursery. The young birds also learned to swim that summer.*

12 | *In Menemsha Harbor, an inspection of the fishing fleet inspires a decision to try...*

3 | What looks like an avant-garde still life makes plain that Penny does not yet have things completely organized.

4 | On the other side of the island, Debbie and Sam, the family dog, get ready to inspect the Bunny Trail at Gay Head.

5 | Down the path to the "wild beach" at Gay Head. The ocean surf there is a little too rough for the girls . . .

8 | . . . where there are good local craftsmen, like this sandal maker. He's cutting leather for a pair . . .

9 | . . . that Penny slipped into right away. An occasional detail shot like this one provides a useful visual change of pace.

10 | Down the street, Kathy and Debbie played with their shadows in the beautiful Methodist Tabernacle in Oak Bluffs.

13 | . . . a little family fishing. Another pre-planned signpost shot announces this turn to a new episode in the story.

14 | The shell-fishing permit is put quickly to work, and of course Mother dug most of the clams out of the mud.

15 | A clambake picnic on the beach was naturally the next order of business. But not all vacation days are sunny, and . . .

16 | . . . sometimes it rains. The view from the front porch is dreary, but little girls will insist on going outside into the rain . . .

17 | . . . and forget to change wet shoes, and catch terrible colds. Happily, Debbie's fever did not last long . . .

18 | . . . and the invalid recovered with servings of chicken soup on the porch.

19 | The vacation nears its end as this slide, another signpost, makes clear. The garage must be cleaned, the telephone bill paid, the man called about the screens . . .

20 | . . . and Penny makes sure that every item is ticked off on the list. She still has to get to work to clean the sink . . .

21 | . . . and take down the curtains in the girls' bedroom and pack them away.

22 | If Sam will get out of the way, it will be possible to finish packing the car . . .

23 | . . . and take the ferry from Vineyard Haven for the sad voyage home. What on earth is the matter with Mommy?

24 | She's crying because they've had such a wonderful summer and now it's over —and so is the show.

The Professional Assignment 5

ALFRED EISENSTAEDT: *Leonard McCombe,* 1964

Photojournalist at Work—A LIFE Photographer's Own Account

Alfred Eisenstaedt once defined the job of a photojournalist in deceptively simple terms. All he has to do, Eisenstaedt said, is "to find and catch the storytelling moment." But to perform this task, the photojournalist needs an extraordinary range of talents and abilities. He must have the instinctive eye for narrative that enabled Margaret Bourke-White, in her first photo essay in LIFE *(pages 63-65),* to bring back a revealing documentary on the hardscrabble life of dam builders at Fort Peck, Montana. He must have the taste for adventure that led George Silk to an ice floe 103 miles from the North Pole to photograph a team of scientists setting up an Arctic weather observation post. He needs the patience and persistence that kept John Dominis eight months on a single assignment photographing giant cats in Africa. He must be able to elbow his way through crowds, past police guards and into situations where he is not always wanted, as when George Skadding sneaked onto a prohibited stretch of beach in Bermuda in 1953 to photograph Winston Churchill, and managed to steal a few telling shots before being carted off by security guards with fixed bayonets. Most important of all, he must have an ability to understand people and a talent for portraying their personalities and emotions. For essentially it is people—their fears, disappointments and triumphs—that make good picture stories.

A deep sensitivity toward people is probably the strongest quality in the work of Leonard McCombe, the LIFE photographer who on the following pages explains how he goes about his job. McCombe's responsiveness illuminates the first of his picture essays to appear in LIFE, a story he shot as a young British photographer in Berlin at the end of World War II. In the aftermath of hostilities, thousands of German refugees were pouring into the Berlin railroad station on top of boxcars—sick, starving, unwanted, and totally unnoticed by most press photographers. McCombe documented their plight in photographs, which he sold first to the London picture weekly *Illustrated.* Henry Luce spotted them, pronounced them the year's best, bought them for the October 15, 1945, issue of LIFE magazine, and ordered that McCombe be hired immediately. McCombe, then 22, became the youngest photographer on the LIFE staff.

McCombe had always been a prodigy in photojournalism. Born on Great Britain's Isle of Man in 1923, he took up photography at age 16 after abandoning an earlier ambition to paint. (His art teacher, in a moment of pedagogical sarcasm, had told him to give up painting and buy a camera.) Within two years, in 1941, McCombe was submitting photographs to London's *Picture Post.* He covered the London blitz during World War II, the Normandy invasion, and earned such a reputation as a war photographer that he was elected to the Royal Photographic Society.

At LIFE McCombe continued to search for the different, more evocative and more significant picture story. One of his first assignments in New York was, of all subjects, the public bathing beach, Jones Beach. "We gave him the biggest cliché we could think of," an editor said later, "to see if he could bring something new to it." McCombe brought back a revelation—not the traditional sea of humanity but intimate portraits of individual humans, each with his own emotions and his own personality.

McCombe's probing type of photography has included all the hazards and hardships that face every photojournalist. In Texas in 1949, while doing a photo essay on cowboys, McCombe returned to the office with the nine-rattle tail of a snake that had been beaten to death a foot in front of him. In Buenos Aires in 1951, while covering Argentine dictator Juan Perón's shutdown of the opposition newspaper *La Prensa,* he was arrested and jailed by secret police, and grilled nonstop for 25 hours until United States and British officials helped to negotiate his release.

Most assignments pose gentler obstacles. Many of the problems are technical: how to get pictures in light that seems too dim, how to find expressive camera angles. More often they are the human problems that McCombe, with his talent for discovering the human elements in a story, solves so well.

In one recent assignment McCombe's sensitivity to people enabled him to develop a story that on the surface seemed impossible to photograph. The editors of LIFE had asked him to shoot an essay on a children's day-care center in Cambridge, Massachusetts. The center was noteworthy because it was one of the first of a number of new child-care facilities around the country to be sponsored in part by industrial firms. KLH, a manufacturer of high-fidelity sound equipment, had started it in 1968 for employees with children under school age. Money was obtained, including a three-year, $324,000 grant for operating expenses from the U.S. Children's Bureau, a building next to the KLH factory was renovated and a staff was recruited. Here, apparently, was a perfect example of big business and government working together to bring about a vitally needed social reform.

But when McCombe arrived at the day-care center, he discovered that the facts had changed. KLH, caught in an economic squeeze, had dropped its support of all but eight of the center's 60 children. The others either paid private tuition, or received help from various outside sources.

For McCombe, the deepest frustration was the fact that the pictures the LIFE editors had presumed could be found—ones that would demonstrate an obvious tie-in between the center and big business—just were not there. But by following his natural instinct for ferreting out the human drama, McCombe managed to bring back other, more evocative photographs that the editors could use to tell their story. How he did it is shown in the account, written by McCombe and illustrated by his pictures, that begins overleaf.

173

Rescuing an "Impossible Project"

Following is Leonard McCombe's story of his "impossible project":

Nearly every assignment seems bewildering when you start—and these pictures showed it. My job was to cover a day-care center sponsored by KLH Research and Development Corporation, Inc., in Cambridge, Massachusetts. It seemed at first glance that there was nothing to photograph: a back lot *(opposite),* a row of swings and a sandbox.

Some small children were playing in groups, and some young teachers were playing with them *(above).* But pictorially it seemed very unexciting.

This is the way it usually happens. You come in cold to an unfamiliar situation, where nobody knows you. The scenes you had imagined often turn out to be nonexistent. "What's going on?" you ask yourself. "Where's my story?" It's like being on the outside of a shop window looking in. Somehow you have to break through the glass.

I looked around for a way to tell the story. There wasn't even a large sign saying "KLH." None of the teachers seemed interested in helping me; they were too busy with their charges. "We had a photographer here last week," one said. "All he did was order us around." From the very start, it looked like an impossible project.

Looking, Listening and Probing for the Story

I saw two ways to approach the problems I faced, and I decided to try them both. First, I would set up the shots that LIFE wanted, hoping to relate the KLH factory and the day-care center *(right)*. I found one of the mothers who worked for KLH, posed her for one picture at her job on the assembly line *(right, below)* and then waving at her 4-year-old daughter from a window of the KLH factory building that overlooked the center's playground *(right, above)*. But as soon as I had taken the pictures I knew that they would look contrived.

Posed pictures never seem to work for me, so I knew I would have to try the second approach: talk to as many people as possible, delving as deeply as I could into the life at the center, in the hope that some special angle would turn up. I went to the center's director, Kate Bulls LaFayette, but she was so busy telephoning *(opposite, above left)* that she had very little time at first to devote to my problems. She was friendly though, and I tagged after her several days in a row, listening and taking photographs as she talked with children and teachers in her office *(opposite, below left)* and the play yard *(opposite, right)*. I did not think the pictures would run, but just the act of shooting them —of framing Kate's face in the viewfinder—helped me understand her intense, forceful personality. I was still groping, but I was beginning to get the feel of the assignment.

An Emerging Quality of Tenderness

Unsatisfied with my attempts to manufacture pictures to order, I resolved to follow my instincts, shooting as many rolls as I had to, hoping to catch something meaningful. I reached the center early in the morning. A light rain was falling. The first person to appear was a social worker, who had bicycled 3 miles through the drizzle with his son *(opposite, left)*. Then I noticed how eager all the children were as they arrived *(opposite, right)*. How many kids in America really *want* to go to school? As I photographed them, I wondered what was so special about the center that made the children so anxious to come.

As the day wore on, I began to pick up clues that helped explain that special quality of the center. I noticed moments of unusual tenderness between the children and the teachers *(above)*. Out of sheer good feeling, a student teacher would pick up a little girl and hug her. Another teacher sat quietly on the asphalt of the playground, cuddling a little boy in her lap.

That night in my hotel room, I realized that a theme was emerging. After a day's shooting, I try to reconstruct each episode I have taken during the day, and to pick out the ones that seemed most meaningful. All my best shots, I felt, showed the remarkable tenderness that existed between the children and their teachers. Now I knew that I had found one theme for the story.

Finding a Way to Dramatize the Theme

In telling a story I use my camera the way a writer uses a typewriter. I take pictures to build a setting and plot. Most of all, I try to develop characters —to make people come alive.

The first character I discovered was five-year-old Jessica Morse, portrayed here in her many moods. I had photographed her by chance on the first day; she sat crying angrily at the edge of the playground *(opposite)*. Soon she acquired a personality. Jessica was not only temperamental, but also intelligent, exuberant and talented. I photographed her pouting as a teacher tried to comfort her *(opposite, right);* painting pictures and smiling at her accomplishment *(above);* and confidently striding out of school at the end of the day with her mother *(right)*.

I had now found a way to dramatize the close rapport between the children and their teachers. For the teachers knew exactly how to respond to Jessica's particular needs and turn her energies toward something positive.

Some of the assignment's initial frustrations had now begun to disappear. The teachers and children started to accept my presence. When a strange photographer first appears to take pictures, most people stop what they are doing and stare at him. This is particularly frustrating, because I like to catch people in an unguarded, characteristic moment. So I try to be as unobtrusive as possible, usually beginning an assignment with a single 35mm camera in order not to frighten people with a lot of complicated equipment. By now the people at the center had lost all their self-consciousness, and I was able to take the kind of spontaneous photographs I wanted.

Catching the Story of a Little Boy

Other personalities intrigued me. One three-year-old boy seemed shy. I first noticed him sitting alone in a corner playing with a hose *(left)*. While his class was in session I watched him —and photographed him—standing by himself on a box in front of a window, swinging his leg *(opposite, left)*. A placard above his head gave the photograph its unusual composition, and his preoccupied expression seemed to tell the essence of his story. The teachers had been striving to bring him out of himself. Eventually he began to make friends with Evie, a little girl his own age, who talked to him, flirted with him and hugged him *(opposite, right)*. "This school is exceptional," his mother said. "My little boy is learning to depend on people—not just to finger paint, but really to trust and share himself. He feels secure here and has such attachments to other children, especially to Evie. He's had to come out of his shell." I began to sense even more strongly how important the center could be in helping children develop.

I also realized something important about the way my assignment was developing. A good photojournalist becomes totally involved in his story. He empathizes with his characters; he develops a point of view and feels a strong desire to express it. I sometimes get so wrapped up in a story that at night I dream about it. I was now beginning to feel this way about the center. Perhaps it was because I have three sons of my own, or perhaps it was simply the drama of watching the children's personalities unfold. In any case I was determined to capture this drama on film so others could understand and sympathize with it as well.

Watching for the Quiet Adventures

For the complete picture of the center I wanted to record all the children's different activities. I took roll after roll of kids eating lunch *(left)*, taking naps *(opposite)*, cavorting about on swings, building castles out of blocks. And I noticed something else about the center. Almost every activity was used as a subtle way of teaching something. At meals, for example, there was a spill-proof milk pitcher that helped even the little girl in the picture at left learn how to pour her own milk.

Photographing nap time was tricky. The teachers did not want to let me do it at first because they were afraid the clicking of the camera shutter would keep the children awake. Even after I had talked them into it, technical problems cropped up. There was almost no light, for example, since the blinds had been pulled down. I tried using a strobe in one shot, but I knew while taking it that the picture would be no good. I hate using strobes because they intrude into the picture, often giving a harsh, artificial light that destroys the air of reality I try to convey. So I went back to natural light. This meant opening my camera to the widest f-stop, and shooting at such a slow shutter speed that I had difficulty keeping the camera steady. A tripod was out—it would only have added another distraction and have kept the children from settling down to sleep.

The nap pictures never really satisfied me, and I went back the following day to get better ones. Finally I caught a scene that seemed to epitomize the soft, human quality I was looking for —the picture opposite of a teacher stroking a little girl's back to make her relax—and I felt I had what I wanted.

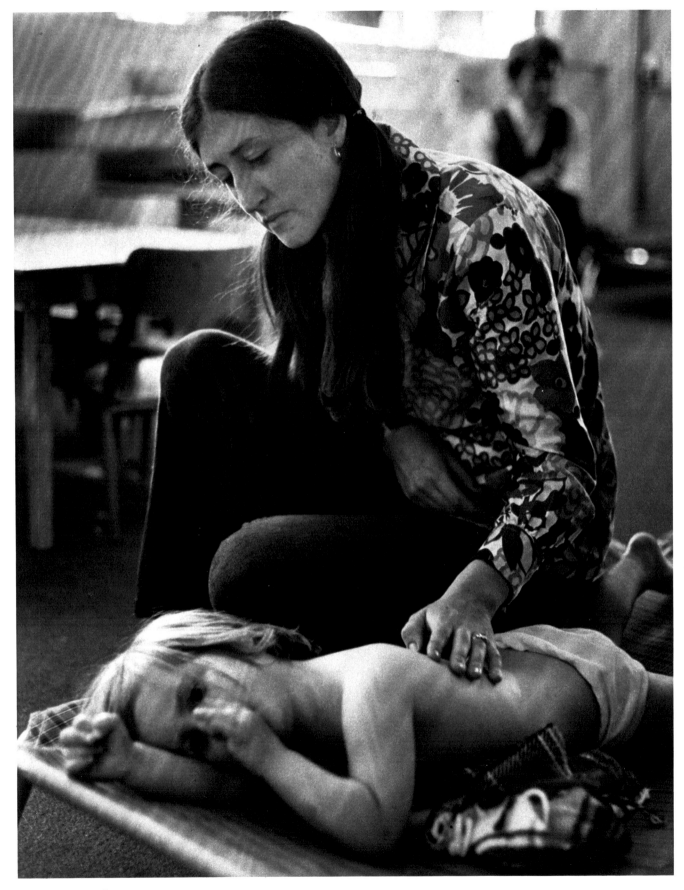

Recording a Scene of Mutual Trust

One of the things that made the center so special, I felt, was the extraordinary sensitivity and dedication of the teachers. I particularly noticed a man with blue jeans and sandals and a huge Afro haircut. His name was Bill Smith, and the children—and their parents—had a deep and total trust in him that I tried to express in the pictures on these pages. The youngsters would cluster around him, holding onto his hand, clutching at his trouser leg or snuggling against him on the couch while he read stories *(opposite, right)*. He could induce them to do whatever he wanted—even to leave the playground to go to class *(opposite, left)* or to wash their hands before lunch *(right, above)*.

Bill Smith seemed to have an unusual gift for understanding each child's personality. I photographed a meeting between parents and teachers one evening after school *(right, bottom)*, and listened as he explained some of the inevitable problems that several children were having in growing up. Afterwards he told me that the success of the center resulted from a sense of trust. "Parents entrust their babies to us," he said. "The kids trust us to be absolutely honest with them. When we are, they are." Bill Smith's young charges exuded this feeling of trust in the pictures I was able to get of them as they followed him around the center.

A Final Success Story

I took my last pictures at a parents' meeting *(above)*. I hoped to capture the enthusiasm that fathers and mothers felt for the center. And, by luck, I managed to dramatize this very point by tying up the threads of an episode I had photographed earlier—pictures indicating the relationship of a teacher to both mother and child *(opposite)*.

Technically, the parents' meeting was very difficult to photograph. I had to climb over people to get the right camera angles, and I made so much noise that I finally took off my shoes. Also, I had to use very slow shutter speeds in the dim light, and I was constantly worried that I might jiggle my camera and blur my shots.

But in one picture I felt I had caught the deep concern of a mother and father *(at right, above)* over their son. Earlier I had photographed the mother embracing one of the teachers, while her young boy looked on *(opposite, right)*. I had no idea what it meant, but it seemed like a significant moment. Then I had photographed the teacher, Mrs.

Lorraine Lee, who was playing a dulcimer *(above)*. At the meeting, I learned that the boy, who had been unhappy, was now far better adjusted, largely because Mrs. Lee and other staff members had broken through to him. It was exactly the kind of success story that explains why the center had become such a valuable social institution.

Result: An Essay with a Twofold Purpose

Director Kate LaFayette, left, watches thoughtfully as ... the day care center's children share morning snacks

Big business tangles with day care problems

Not far from the shadow of dark factory walls, Jessica Morse tilts crazily on a swing, lively children grab for orange juice and apples, and little Bobby Cunningham (right), at 7 in the morning, races to his teacher. Some children their age, were it not for the KLH Child Development Center in Cambridge, Mass., might have been cooped up in an apartment with—or even without—a parent. To them, from 6:45 to 5:30, the center is not only a school but a comfortable daytime home, never to be confused, the center's teachers say, with a parking lot for kids.

The need for day care centers is critical and growing: six million children under 6 have mothers who have jobs, but there are only 640,000 places in licensed centers to accommodate them. KLH, maker of high-fidelity sound equipment, started this center two years ago as an experiment in industrial sponsorship. Designed to provide all-day year-round care for children 2½ to 6, its purpose was to make jobs possible for blue-collar workers who, without day care arrangements, might have to stay home with their children and subsist at a poverty level. The workers' children, paid for by them and KLH, were later joined by others whose parents could pay all of the $37.50 weekly cost, and by children of welfare families, paid for by the state. The center set out not only to offer a sound program of preschool education, but to serve as a pilot model for industry at large.

Now the center's original two-year HEW grant has expired. Ironically, the general economic pinch has cut down on the number of children KLH can support. This year all but 10 of the school's 60 children come from either middle-class or welfare families; 15 are from MIT's staff. But this mixture of backgrounds is proving a real success and, with or without funds from HEW and KLH, the center expects to continue at full steam. "We are probably ahead of our times," says Director Kate LaFayette, "but we represent something that is desperately needed."

Photographed by **LEONARD McCOMBE**

My photographs of the KLH Child Development Center ran for three spreads in LIFE, on July 31, 1970, with my by-line on the first spread (above). Looking back on it, I found that I had put in 40 difficult, frustrating man-hours; I had shot a total of 1,500 negatives (far too many, it seems in retrospect); I had to cope with some nasty technical and journalistic hurdles. I had been able to give only the barest suggestion of the connection between the day-care center and industry that the editors had asked for. But the editors used the text to describe the relationship, and the financial problems, between the center and KLH and they used my pictures in another way that was also fundamental to the story—to make clear in interesting and human terms why the center itself is an important social institution. ☐

Leonard McCombe

190

The Ubiquitous Photograph 6

Photojournalism's Media–Cards to Posters

Ultimately, the mark of success for any photojournalist is to get his pictures published. For reporting with a camera, like writing for a newspaper, is a kind of communication between the journalist and his audience. The moments of reality that the photographer traps on film, whether spot news pictures of home-town election campaigns or exotic travelogues, communicate nothing to anyone if they are stored away in an attic trunk.

Most people think of photojournalism as being limited to the pictures that get published in newspapers and national magazines. But journalistic photographs—ones that tell a story or report on some aspect of reality—are everywhere. They appear on calendars and postcards, adorn book jackets and record covers, and illustrate posters and travel brochures.

Long before the first photograph could be printed in the press, in fact, the early photographers were taking—and marketing—pictures that were unquestionably journalistic. Mathew Brady sold his thousands of Civil War pictures not only for reproduction in magazines (which converted the photographs into woodcuts for printing, since no facsimile process had yet been invented), but directly to the general public in the form of actual prints. Brady's chief competitor, Alexander Gardner, published picture albums in which his Civil War prints were glued to each page by hand.

An even richer vehicle for the mass distribution of pictures was provided by card photographs. They were first used in 1857 in Italy by the Duke of Parma, who pasted miniature portraits of himself on his calling cards. Soon, enterprising photographers in Europe and America were mass-producing similar cards with portraits of famous people, such as politicians, prize fighters, actresses and acrobats. In the Midwest, particularly fast-selling items were souvenir cards of captured outlaws, portrayed either dead or alive, with all their wounds and battle scars. When several members of the Jesse James gang were brought to heel after a gun battle with Minnesota lawmen in 1876, a local photographer took pictures of the captives, three of whom were now corpses, and within a month had sold 50,000 prints. But this was smalltime stuff compared with the business generated by the major distributors back East. One photographic firm, E. and H. T. Anthony and Company of New York (a predecessor of Ansco), churned out as many as 3,600 prints a day of various celebrities. Studio portraits always outnumbered the more journalistic subjects on the cards. But in the days before newspaper photography, they were almost the only means by which most Americans learned to recognize the faces of the people who made news.

One medium exceeded all the others as a marketplace for the work of early photojournalists. This was a device called the stereoscope, a standard fixture in almost every Victorian parlor. It created the illusion of three dimensions by using two prints of the same subject, taken from slightly different angles and placed side by side on a card. When looked at through the stereoscope, the two views merged into a single, lifelike image. And what a wide new world the stereoscope brought home to its 19th Century viewers! The snow-capped parapets of the Alps, the stones and deserts of the Holy Land, the scowling Indians of the Wild West, the smoke and suffering of the Civil War. And the news of the day. In 1860 alone, six years after Langenheim Brothers of Philadelphia introduced the first stereoscopic pictures to the United States, stereoscopic cameras recorded the arrival in New York of the century's largest steamship, the *Great Eastern;* the American visit of Queen Victoria's heir, Edward, Prince of Wales; and the welcome of the first diplomatic mission from Japan, which provided many Americans with their first glimpse of Japanese people, and also provided the enterprising Japanese with their first good look at a camera.

The Victorian world was enthralled. Oliver Wendell Holmes, who himself designed one version of the stereoscope in 1859, pronounced the medium "a leaf torn from the book of God's recording angel," and proceeded to assemble an immense collection of stereoscopic cards. The rest of the world was not far behind. The London Stereoscopic Company of Great Britain, founded in 1854 and one of the first distributors, was selling almost a million stereographs a year by 1862. The leading American firm, E. and H. T. Anthony, started late (1859) with a list of only 175 views. But within two years its annual sales had reached several hundred thousand cards.

The rage for the stereoscope lingered on through the turn of the century. Sears, Roebuck sought a final piece of the action, listing views for as little as 40 cents a dozen in its 1897 mail-order catalogue—not "the cheap, trashy printed views, but only those on the regular photographic paper from a negative." The Spanish-American War provided a brief Indian summer for the medium, and cards of the San Francisco earthquake of 1906 sold well. But with the increasing use of photographs in newspapers and magazines, the fad began to die, and photojournalists turned to other outlets for their work.

Today, journalistic photographs appear in more places and under more different guises than ever before. Picture buyers increasingly rely on their look of candid realism to catch the attention of audiences. Advertising companies use photojournalistic techniques to lend immediacy and naturalism to their ad campaigns. Picture essays, following patterns established by LIFE and other magazines, enliven the pages of trade journals, company house organs and special-interest magazines. Each medium has its special requirements—calendar makers want pictures that show the time of year, book jackets suggest the volume's content. But in every case, the basic techniques of photojournalism remain the same, communicating to the public the moments of reality captured by the reporter with a camera.

Greeting Cards at Home and Abroad

Ever since tourists first sent home views of the Grand Canyon and the Swiss Alps, people have been mailing picture postcards *(opposite)* from all over the world to their friends. Like the stereoscopic pictures of the past, the cards document the look and the atmosphere of far-off places. And as with the stereographs, the volume of business is gigantic. One of the largest postcard firms in America, Dexter Press, publishes 50,000 different views a year, and sells up to 500 million cards.

Photographs have begun to give a new look to the greeting-card business as well. In the past, card companies have used pictures of snowy landscapes or spruce trees on Christmas cards. But recently several inventive entrepreneurs have turned to a kind of moody naturalism to convey messages of tenderness and immediacy. "We pick photographs by intuition—by gut feel," explained Mel Marshall, who founded Empathy Graphics in 1969 and within a year had sold 4,000,000 cards. "The only requirement is that the photograph say something."

Photographic greeting cards convey a mood or a message. David Fitzgerald's soft-focus dandelions (above, left) suggested the freshness of early morning to the American Greetings Corporation. Jack Zehrt's Hawaiian surfer, bought by Empathy Graphics, rides the curl of a seemingly endless giant wave.

Journalistic postcards report to the folks at home from far-off places: a gondolier in Venice's flooded Piazza San Marco (top, left); women grinding grain and an elephant in Africa (top, center and right); traffic in, and over, Greece's Corinth Canal (bottom, left); and folk dancing in the Canary Islands (bottom, right).

197

Calendar Art from the Camera

One specialized user of photographs is the calendar publisher, who prefers photographs with a strong decorative sense, since his product is usually designed to be hung on walls. Often the calendar publisher chooses a picture that reflects a particular time of year. In the Swiss calendar at right a regatta of sailboats on a mountain lake illustrates a week in July, while the mountains dominating the picture bespeak Switzerland, where even in summer the highest peaks are snow-capped.

Because most calendars publicize something—a country, a company, a product or a point of view—calendar publishers also try to emphasize this point with their pictures. The National Audubon Society is dedicated to preserving American wildlife; so the cover of its calendar *(opposite)* features a picture of a threatened species: an Alaskan brown bear fishing in a rushing Alaskan stream.

JULI	JUILLET	LUGLIO	JULY
9	SONNTAG / DIMANCHE / DOMENICA / SUNDAY		
10	MONTAG / LUNDI / LUNEDÌ / MONDAY		
11	DIENSTAG / MARDI / MARTEDÌ / TUESDAY		
12	MITTWOCH / MERCREDI / MERCOLEDÌ / WEDNESDAY		
13	DONNERSTAG / JEUDI / GIOVEDÌ / THURSDAY		
14	FREITAG / VENDREDI / VENERDÌ / FRIDAY		
15	SAMSTAG / SAMEDI / SABATO / SATURDAY		

Segelregatta auf dem Silvaplanersee. Piz La Margna
Régate sur le lac de Silvaplana. Piz La Margna
Regata di barche a vela sul lago di Silvaplana. Pizzo La Margna
Sailing regatta on the Lake of Silvaplana. Piz La Margna
Regata sobre el lago de Silvaplana. Pico la Margna

The Photo-Almanach Suisse is a photographic travelogue that documents the changes in the Swiss landscape week by week throughout the year. Photographer Louis Beringer, who is also the calendar's publisher, evokes July with this picture of small racing craft on an Alpine lake.

Photographer Leonard Lee Rue took 2,000 negatives in shooting a series of pictures of Alaskan brown bear, one of which (opposite) was used by the National Audubon Society on its calendar. Since the bears are dangerous, Rue kept his distance, using a long lens, carrying a pistol or a hunting rifle for protection, and positioning himself under a rocky overhang to guard against attack from the rear.

AUDUBON 1971 CALENDAR

The Big Business of Company Magazines

Among the most omnivorous users of journalistic photographs are company magazines. Their number is large, and they range from newsy tabloids full of pictures and chatty anecdotes about employees and their families to sophisticated quarterlies that contain articles on various current issues and picture essays modeled on those in LIFE or *Look.* Some are distributed internally to employees, and some are sent out to stockholders, clients, business leaders and the general public.

House organs are almost as old as industry itself. America's first was probably the *Lowell Offering,* started in the 1840s in Massachusetts by the Lowell Cotton Mills, a pioneer in mass pro-duction techniques. Another pioneer, Henry Ford, rolled out the first issue of the long-lived *Ford Times* in 1908, the same year that the first Model T rolled off the production line. *Ford Times* re-lied on photography, then a new tech-nique in magazines, to show the look of the company's new cars.

Today, the editors of house organs continue to use the most professional editorial techniques to catch the at-tention of their readers. "We try to put out a publication with a handsome and contemporary design," says James O'Connell, editor of IBM's magazine *THINK.* And part of the design, for most house organs, includes the realism and immediacy of good photojournalism.

Each issue of Old Bullion, published intermittently by New York's Chemical Bank for its 12,500 employees, is devoted to various aspects of company business. Usually the theme is developed as a picture essay, as in this feature on bank tellers that included a spread (above) on how new tellers are trained.

Alcoans This Month

Making the Hullabaloo Scene

Davenport (Iowa) Works Mill Maintenance Foreman John Boesch invites adults to make the *Hullabaloo Scene*, provided they don't stay long.

"We want to keep *Hullabaloo* strictly for teen-agers," he explained.

Mr. Boesch is part owner of the *Hullabaloo Scene*, a teen spot in Moline, Ill., that's off limits for everyone under age 13 and over 30. "You have to understand the nature of being young and needing a place where you and your friends can be together doing what everybody likes," said Mr. Boesch. "That's the kind of place we think *Hullabaloo* should be." *Hullabaloo Scene* is open once a week during the school year and on special holidays. Openings are scheduled around school activities. Entertainment is live: rock bands that attract the young in droves. The drinks aren't stronger than soda pop. Lights flash on and off. Sound beats on the crowd through giant amplifiers. The youngsters love it, and for Moline teens, *Hullabaloo* is "where everything's at."

All of which makes John Boesch a proud man.

He will never see 30 again, but for someone who is supposedly beyond the age to understand young people, John Boesch seems to have hit on one way to fulfill their needs.

Suriname Alcoans Race for International Stakes

Seven two-man teams from Suralco—Alcoa's mining, refining and smelting subsidiary in Suriname, South America—took part in the first international auto rally between Suriname and neighboring French Guiana last February.

Although the day-long competition was won by a French crew, Leo Tjong Ayong (left) and Bill Johnson, both electrical engineers at Paranam, led the other Suralco teams in their front-wheel-drive, Japanese-made car. The duo averaged 33 miles an hour (14 miles per gallon) along a 400-mile racecourse—the two-lane highway connecting Cayenne, the capitol of French Guiana, with Paramaribo.

"Much of the road was paved, but portions were only gravel, and other parts were just packed earth," said Mr. Tjong Ayong. "In places it was not possible to pass, especially where the road went through the jungle.

"Almost every team experienced some difficulty—shattered windshields or headlights, broken carburetors, flat and smashed tires, and lost mufflers. But considering these conditions, everyone was very lucky. All 38 teams finished under their own power."

The Suralco cars did capture one honor, however. It was the "Turtle Prize"—awarded to the unluckiest driver-navigator pair.

Leo Tjong Ayong predicts a better showing for Suriname in next year's race. "We're going to win," he said. "And it will be a Suralco team that wins first prize."

Carlena Competes

Eighteen-year-old Carlena Reed, daughter of 29-year Alcoan John Reed, a property agent at Arkansas Operations, competed last month for the "Miss Arkansas" title in Hot Springs. In an earlier competition in her hometown—Benton—the musically talented miss was named "Miss Benton of 1970"—a win which made her eligible to try for the state title.

Carlena is employed by the operations' purchasing department this summer, but plans to attend the University of Arkansas as a sophomore in the fall. She will major in education with piano and voice instruction.

Teacher-to-be Spurs Team to Title

When the St. Clair High School basketball team ran away with the Pennsylvania state championship earlier this year, Cressona (Pa.) Works Alcoan Mike Buletza had good reason to be proud. His son, Matt, was on the starting five.

The six-foot, 17-year-old athlete admitted he never really believed his team could win the state trophy—at least not in the beginning. But Mike Buletza—a basketball player himself during his school days—thought differently. "I figured they had the ability to go all the way," said the elder Buletza, a fabricating machine operator and 18-year Alcoan. "They're a good bunch, and they didn't let up, ever."

The St. Clair five got off to a good start by copping the North Schuylkill League title. Then the team chalked up playoff wins over Jim Thorpe, Schuylkill Haven, Darby, Mt. Penn, and Northwest, until only Laurel Valley stood between St. Clair and victory.

"We felt we just had to go out on that floor and do our best. The seniors knew it was their last game," explained Matt, "and the juniors and sophomores felt they might never again get a chance at a state championship. So, we gave it all we had."

The St. Clair five walked away from Laurel Valley 76-55 to cinch the trophy.

Matt Buletza's new goal is a college degree in elementary education at Lock Haven State College.

"That's the main thing as far as I'm concerned," said his father. "I want to see him get his education."

18

19

A regular department of The Alcoa News, distributed monthly to the 50,000 employees of the Aluminum Company of America, is a section that describes the activities of employees. The editors try to use informal, candid photographs like the basketball picture at right.

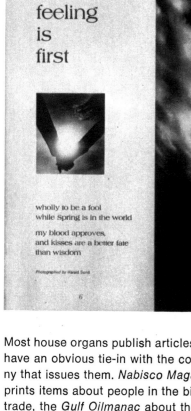

feeling is first

wholly to be a fool
while Spring is in the world

my blood approves,
and kisses are a better fate
than wisdom

Photographed by Harald Sund

6

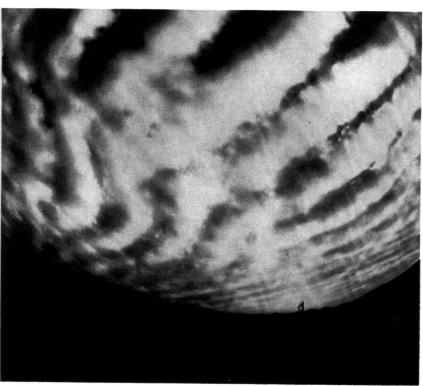

we are for each other: then
laugh, leaning back in my arms
for life's not a paragraph

Most house organs publish articles that have an obvious tie-in with the company that issues them. *Nabisco Magazine* prints items about people in the biscuit trade, the *Gulf Oilmanac* about the petroleum business. But some magazines, such as Pacific Northwest Bell's *Cascades,* run photographs and stories that have a much broader appeal. *Cascades,* which is read by a large general audience in Washington, Oregon and Idaho, treats such issues as race relations and pollution, and prints photographs that show the natural beauty of the Northwest. "We try to talk honestly and well about whatever topic we pick, and so gain good will for the phone company," says a staffer. "If the subject is well served, so is the company."

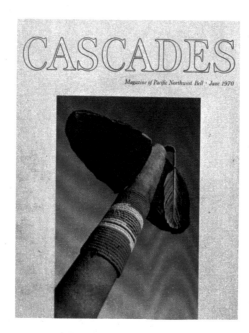

CASCADES

Magazine of Pacific Northwest Bell · June 1970

In the June 1970 issue of Cascades, an editorial on environment was followed by an evocative picture essay (above, center) of two young people in wide open spaces, photographed by freelance Harald Sund. The only text was from a poem by e. e. cummings. "We tried to show photographically the resources—both natural and human—that are worth preserving," one spokesman said. The issue's cover (left) featured an Indian tomahawk, photographed by Sund, heralding a story on Indian artifacts.

ath I think is no parenthesis.

– e. e. cummings

Special Pictures for Special Publications

that day is coming when Jackson will join the softer, gentler, prettier world of the American skier. But that, alone, will not banish the rugged, ragged band; rather, the body ages, caution creeps in where only daring lived before, and a certain "maturity" tempers the heedless risks of youth. But the couloirs will remain for the new wild bunch —and those who felt the freedom will never forget. **SKI**

The Jackson Ski Patrol blasts an overhanging cornice from the Corbet Couloir, above left. A man can put courage and skill to the test, above, by jumping straight into the Corbet Couloir and hoping to stop by skidturning on the nearly vertical slope. Few land without a fall. Jimmy Stanton, lower left, wooshes off.

SKI, SEPTEMBER 1970   SKI SEPTEMBER 1970

The daredevil capers of schussbooming skiers at Jackson Hole, Wyoming, caught at the critical moment by sports photographer Del Mulkey, made a spread in a picture essay for the September 1970 issue of Ski magazine.

Most of the world's magazines never reach the newsstands, or if they do are bought only by very select, single-minded readers. These are trade journals and special interest magazines that cater to almost every conceivable audience, from antelope hunters to amateur zoologists. Magazines for animal lovers run from *The American Dachshund* to *The Western Horseman*. Religious publications include such evocative titles as *Eternity* (for conservative Protestants) and the Salvation Army's *The War Cry*. Farmers can snuggle down with *Soybean Digest, Grain Age, Electricity On The Farm*, the *Dairy Goat Journal*, or *Gobbles* (for turkey breeders). And for officials in city government there are such periodicals as *The National Sheriff, Fire Station Digest*, or the *Solid Wastes Management/Refuse Removal Journal*.

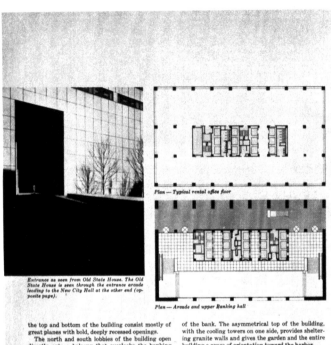

Entrance as seen from Old State House. The Old State House is seen through the entrance arcade leading to the New City Hall at the other end (opposite page).

Plan — Typical rental office floor

Plan — Arcade and upper Banking hall

the top and bottom of the building consist mostly of great planes with bold, deeply recessed openings.

The north and south lobbies of the building open directly onto a balcony that overlooks the banking hall and leads to the elevators. The banking hall, with tellers ranged under the balcony and executive desks under the high east windows, is entirely faced with granite. At each end are huge historical murals by Larry Rivers — the Ride of Paul Revere and the Boston Massacre. The cross light on the end walls makes one aware of the whole volume of the base.

The restaurant-club is a terraced room with tables on separate levels all having a view down to Boston Harbor. It is a cavelike space behind a deep portico that softens the glare of the sky. Curtains are unnecessary. Barnes feels that ". . . the all too obvious panoramic rooftop restaurant should be avoided. In fact, on a rooftop more than anywhere, one welcomes a sense of enclosure and framed view."

The roof garden above the restaurant serves two private-duplex floors which are the executive offices

of the bank. The asymmetrical top of the building, with the cooling towers on one side, provides sheltering granite walls and gives the garden and the entire building a sense of orientation toward the harbor.

The building contributes variety to the pedestrian ways of Government Center. It is sited to provide a little square in front of the Old State House and to expose the Richardsonian façade of the Ames Building. The high arcade at the base is not placed facing the Old State House in an obviously dominating way but along one side of the building flanking Washington Street, which the Boston Redevelopment Authority has designated as a pedestrian way. Thus, the arcade becomes a monumental passage from the old neighborhood to the new City Hall Plaza.

Instead of setting the building on a podium, architect Barnes accepted and exploited the site, which slopes down to the underpass under the City Hall Plaza on the City Hall and Washington Street sides. On these two sides, the solid base of the building is a pivot; the heavy vehicular traffic of Congress Street

Many of these publications use photojournalism to add sparkle to their pages. In each case the pictures relate closely to the reader's special interest. Sports magazines, such as *Ski (opposite),* favor dramatic shots of athletes in motion. But even in architectural journals, such static subjects as the glass and steel of new buildings *(above)* come to life when seen through the reportorial eye of photojournalism.

Boston's new office skyscraper, the 40-story New England Merchants National Bank Building, stimulated Progressive Architecture magazine in 1970 to report on it in photographs. The editors included shots (above, left) from the outside looking in by Michel Proulx and from the inside looking out by Ted Gorchev (above, right).

Describing a Book with Its Cover

All India, from the guru on his elephant to the pilgrim with his ashes, seems present in this book cover picture by Marilyn Silverstone.

For a sociological study of American Indians Penguin Books chose this vignette of modern life on a Blackfeet reservation in Montana.

Like cereal boxes and candy wrappers, book covers (or dust jackets as they are called in the trade) are a kind of packaging, designed to catch the attention of potential buyers. And like all good packaging, they must indicate the contents. Fiction covers, for example, are often illustrated by imaginative drawings that depict the main characters or dramatic moments in the plot. But for nonfiction works—documentaries, biographies, politics, education—publishers frequently turn to journalistic photographs to convey a feeling of un-adorned veracity. Farrar, Straus & Giroux, the publishers of Ved Mehta's *Portrait of India (above),* sifted through hundreds of photographs to find an appropriate cover.

"The author himself chose the one we finally used," said publisher Robert Giroux. It was taken in 1960 during a Hindu festival at Allahabad. "Besides its beautiful composition and unusual lighting, it communicates the essence of the India the author describes—its mystery, its religion, its multitudes of people from all castes of society."

Scenarios of the Revolution

DO IT!
Jerry Rubin
Introduction by
ELDRIDGE CLEAVER

Jerry Rubin's call to revolution has one of the
author's favorite photographs as a cover. It was
taken originally for LIFE by Rowland Scherman.

I Learn From Children
Caroline Pratt

Cornerstone Library

Reissuing a noted work on progressive
education, Cornerstone Library used this picture
of children at play by Richard Bluestein.

Leon Harris
THE RUSSIAN
BALLET SCHOOL

Leon Harris selected this portrait for the cover
of his pictorial documentary of Russian children
learning ballet, published by Atheneum.

Conveying the Mood of Music

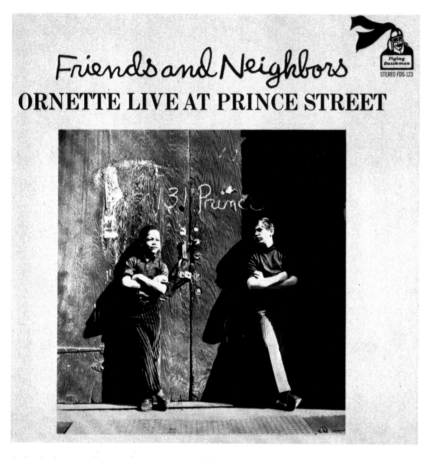

A disc by jazzman Ornette Coleman, recorded live in New York City, has a cover of youngsters photographed on location by Ray Ross.

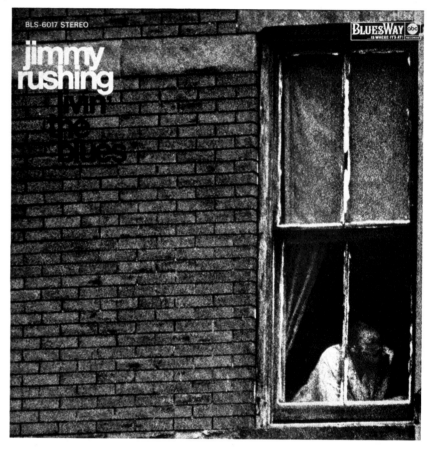

To evoke the quiet desolation of Jimmy Rushing's blues sound, ABC Records' William Duevell took this shot of a woman in Harlem.

Record covers, like book jackets, provide a visual metaphor of the subject matter inside them. Whether examples of graphic art or photographs, they at least suggest something about the music—its mood, its style and perhaps the personality of its performer.

To boost sales, record companies continually strive for jackets that grab attention. Sometimes they try to shock. Apple Corps. Ltd., which records the Beatles, caused a transatlantic brouhaha in 1968, when it issued *The Two* *Virgins* in a jacket that showed John Lennon and his future wife Yoko Ono explicitly portrayed in the nude. But graphic realism can also be pristinely photojournalistic. "I abhor sensationalism," says David Gahr, who shot a record jacket for a 1964 Newport Folk Festival album for Vanguard *(opposite, left).* "My purpose is to document the folk scene—to photograph what's there in a totally candid way. I never interfere with the scene. I let it reveal itself before the camera lens."

VANGUARD Recordings for the Connoisseur   STEREOLAB VSD-79182

TRADITIONAL MUSIC at NEWPORT 1964 Part 1
Recorded Live at the Newport Folk Festival July 23-26

Hobart Smith ✳ Moving Star Hall Singers ✳ Sarah Gunning ✳ Cajun Band
Willy Doss ✳ Ken & Neriah Benfield ✳ Sacred Harp Singers ✳ Chet Parker and Elgia Hickok
Joe Patterson ✳ Bill Thatcher ✳ Doc Watson (WITH GAITHER CARLTON & ARNOLD WATSON) ✳ Fred MacDowell

*David Gahr's cover for an album of folk music
recorded at Newport shows the Victorian
cottage where many of the musicians stayed.*

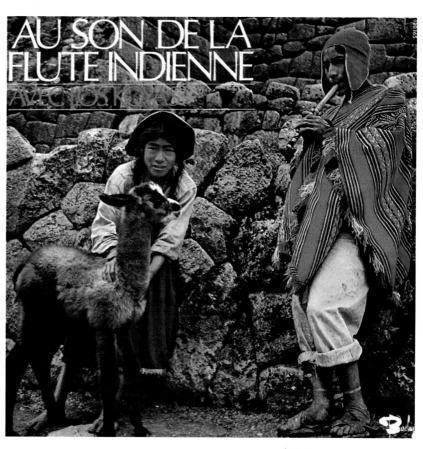

AU SON DE LA FLUTE INDIENNE

*France's Barclay Records chose these Peruvian
shepherds, taken by Michel Hétier near Cuzco,
for a disc of South American flute music.*

Helping Corporations Look Their Best

Stacks of Metalbestos gas vent pipes in varying sizes. These advanced designs assure flow of flue gases without draft/hood spillage. Lightweight stacks capped with weatherproof "Belmont tops" are parts of venting systems for homes, commercial buildings and industrial plants.

Below: Subdued glow of light reflecting inside barrels of all-stainless steel chimney sections stacked at a warehouse for shipment to plants or homes where they will replace brick chimneys. These factory-built units are made in diameters from 6 to 14 inches in 2½-foot sections that can be quickly stacked and locked. They may revolutionize this aspect of building.

Right: Reflections of light from out edges of aluminum gas vent pipes. These Metalbestos parts are ready to be assembled. They will be packaged and shipped for use in apartment houses, buildings and factories.

Publishing an annual report, according to one skittish businessman from overseas, is like "being forced to undress in public." Over the years the big American corporations have become adept at presenting the best possible appearance even when revealing their intimate financial secrets. They dress up their annual reports in the latest styles in photographic artwork, spending over $75 million a year, or between 50 cents and one dollar a copy, to give the reports a slick, contemporary look. "An annual report does not merely compete with other annual reports for attention, but also with LIFE, *National Geographic* and *Playboy*," claims Leslie A. Segal, co-founder of Corporate Annual Reports, Inc., a firm that specializes in

designing reports for other companies.

To help keep stockholders' attention, the publishers of annual reports usually play down the production graphs and balance sheets and play up the pictures and text to present a photojournalistic portrait of the company. Photographs range from portraits of top executives to depictions of products in use *(opposite, top)*, abstract photographs of products *(above)* or even of production lines. As in a good picture essay, the photographs tell a story, in this case one that enhances the basic purpose of the report—to present the company in the best possible light for its stockholders, its clients, and, not least, to the Wall Street analysts who influence the price of the company's stock.

The Wallace-Murray Corporation wanted to give its annual report a futuristic look that emphasized the manufacturing firm's advances in research and technology. Photographer Simpson Kalisher's pictures seem almost like abstractions: at left above, a device used to test the hardness of metals, and, at center and right, stacks of vents and chimney sections.

To show the many operations of Bangor Punta, a ▶ holding company that makes everything from sailboats to police revolvers, the firm's annual report included photographs of company products in action. In the top picture opposite, a policeman notes the speed of a passing car on a dashboard computer made by a Bangor Punta division. Another holding company, Norlin Corporation, indicated its activities in South America with a picture of a worker operating a malt kiln in Ecuador (opposite, below).

Through Smith & Wesson's Public Security group, Bangor Punta meets today's universal need for improved safety and modern law enforcement. Here, the speed of a passing automobile is registered in miles-per-hour on the digital readout of a TDS Speed Computer. Sophisticated devices like this are being used in increasing number to help stem the tide of highway deaths.

14

15

The Company's program to encourage independent local farmers to grow barley has been very successful—resulting in a record crop for malting purposes during 1968.

Operations in South America

During the 55 years our Company has operated in Ecuador, we have found the business climate to be favorable, the economy stable, and the currency sound —in fact, the Ecuadorian sucre is one of the sound currencies of the world. The economy has grown steadily, if modestly, over those years. However, since the discovery of large quantities of oil in the Northeastern Provinces in 1967, the economic growth rate has begun to increase. While it may be five years or more before the oil actually begins to flow to the coast by pipeline, exploration and development activity is generating employment and income. We believe the future growth of the Ecuadorian economy should be more rapid than in the past; and, accordingly, we are expanding all of our major operations there.

CONSTRUCTION MATERIALS

During the first quarter of 1968, cement manufacturing capacity was increased 50%. But demand has continued to expand during 1968 so that, during the last half, the cement plant was again operating at 100% of capacity. Cement sales during 1968 increased 20% over 1967. While La Cemento Nacional experiences important competition from two other cement mills in the country, LCN enjoys a reputation for uniformly high quality cement.

In 1968 Ecuador completed its first major cement highway, 26 miles long. Ecuador is currently engaged in a major road building program, financed in part by international agencies, which should continue to exert a favorable influence upon cement sales.

Concrete block production by Productos Rocafuerte achieved new records with a sales advance of 19% over 1967. Housing and public works contractors, as well as the general

Journalism in Advertising

In Jamaica, you can sail a 19th century rum-smuggling ship over seas that hide 16th century Spanish gold and a 17th century sunken city.

The "Caribee" still sails with a load of rum on. (Daiquiris. Planter's punches. Swizzles.)

Board at midday and whip into the blue, sails billowing, mahogany decks swaying, feeling like Douglas Fairbanks, Sr.

Swashbuckle. Sun. Raise a tankard or two. Get back in time for dinner. Drunk with the past.

The gold? You can scuba to hunt for it yourself. But, these days, finders *not* keepers. To the government go the spoils.

The loot you *can* take home is counterfeit. Pewter copies of coins from Port Royal, our watery Pompeii.

The city, once pirate Henry Morgan's treasury, slid into the sea from an earthquake 275 years ago as "retribution for his sins."

Today, it's being dug up. And duplicated. (Pirate-era spoons, jars, plates look like new again.)

Though piracy is *out,* adventuring is still *in* in Jamaica.

Explore our "jungle" (Cockpit Country), a thicket of strange mounds that "look like women's bosoms all covered in green." Meet our Maroon "tribesmen." See them dance a wild quadrille.

Spelunk.

Hunt boars.

Race in a motor rally.

Scale Blue Mountain. By mule, then foot, huffing and puffing the last steep 6 miles after midnight to reach the top in time to see the sun rise. Whew. Wow.

For less exciting things to do, see your local travel agent or Jamaica Tourist Board in New York, San Francisco, Miami, Chicago, Los Angeles, Toronto, Montreal.

One of the richest markets for journalistic photographs is in advertising. Ad agencies occasionally pay as much as $1,000 for the right pictures.

Most advertising photographs are shot in the studio or on location with posed models. But a significant number show unadorned moments of real life, caught by the candid techniques of photojournalism. The result is a dividend in freshness and believability that studio photographs seldom achieve.

Some ad campaigns use photojournalism to copy the editorial style of magazines, on the theory that people are more likely to react to advertisements that look like editorial matter than to obvious advertisements. "We wanted something that would convey the history and romance of Jamaica," said the copywriter for the sailing ship ad above. "At the same time we wanted something that would match the editorial quality of LIFE magazine."

A venerable cargo schooner (above), caught under sail in the rolling waters off Montego Bay by Belgian photojournalist Robert Freson, adorns this advertisement created by Doyle Dane Bernbach, Inc., in a campaign for the Jamaica Tourist Board.

International Ladies' Garment Workers' Union used this news photo taken during ...er-registration drive in Georgia as a way ...natize the importance of voting—and, by ...tion, the voting power of the union itself.

A pole vaulter in mid-leap, photographed ...y Ernst Haas, was used by General Mills to advertise the powerful qualities assertedly provided by the company's natural vitamin E concentrates.

...demonstrate its public-spirited concern over education, the Addressograph-Multigraph Corporation featured a high-school dropout photographed in a Cleveland, Ohio, alleyway by Jan Czyrba.

The walk to the Registrar's Office was the easy part.

The tough part was deciding to take the walk. Jim Dyous knew that out there was a townful of people who didn't want him to register; didn't want him to vote. People who'd prevented him from registering for 60 years. People who would, if they could, make him sorry he took that walk. He walked. He registered. He voted.

That's all there was to it. You don't have Jim's problems. If you're 21 you have the right to vote. And you won't find people hanging around the registration office letting *you* know that *they* know what you're doing.

You don't have any excuses. If you've registered you have the right to vote.

If you don't vote—you get who's coming to you.

This message has been sponsored by the International Ladies' Garment Workers' Union—who through their union, and by their votes—have won dignity, fair wages and decent working conditions. Join us.

Supercharged E

He might have been the man who discovered a cure for cancer.

Dropouts become losers.
They lose.
And we lose.
Today's dropouts might have been tomorrow's scientists. Or doctors. Or teachers.
But what might have been will never be.
For one out of three high school students doesn't stick around to graduate.
The dropout is ten times as likely to become a juvenile delinquent.
And the juvenile delinquent is perhaps a thousand times more likely to become a criminal.
It doesn't have to happen.
Good schools with good teachers and good facilities can produce good citizens. And that can make our world a better place in which to live.
Which is why money spent on education represents the best investment we can make.
An investment in the future of America.

This message is sponsored by the Copier Duplicator and VariTyper divisions of the Addressograph Multigraph Corporation.

As businessmen who have a stake in education.

First, because we are deeply involved in ways to use communications technology to improve the quality of American education. (For instance, the Multilith offset press has been used in programs that serve to recapture the interest of potential high school dropouts and help prepare them for gainful employment.)

Second, because we believe America's future—and ours—is no better than the future of American education.

If you would like more information on how educators are using the products of the Copier Duplicator and VariTyper divisions to improve their schools—or if you'd like reprints of this message—write Addressograph Multigraph Corporation, 1200 Babbitt Road, Cleveland, Ohio 44117. (Information sources on request.)

All the local color a railroad traveler could see
for only 130 marks made up the layout
for this Deutsche Bundesbahn advertisement.

Convenience was the theme of this ad.
Railroad stations are easy to get to, at the heart
of each city, said the accompanying text.

"Window seat. Was it luck? Nein. Reservation,"
proclaimed the headline, stressing one of the
services offered to Bundesbahn passengers.

The editorial look in advertising was used as long ago as 1926, when the Pennsylvania Railroad ran a series of photojournalistic ads that told the story, in dramatic and human terms, of the line operation. One of the most striking modern examples of this device was its use in 1966 by West Germany's Deutsche Bundesbahn (West German Railroad) in an attempt to improve its image with German travelers.

For several years the German railroad had been losing customers to the automobiles. To win them back it hired McCann-Erickson, which devised a campaign attempting to demonstrate that train travel was safer, faster, more convenient and more fun than fighting traffic on the *Autobahnen.* Each individual ad in the series used pictures and text to develop a single theme—for example, the fact that a tourist could see much of West Germany by train for only 130 marks, or about 30 dollars *(above, left).* And even in series the ads told a story, functioning as spreads in an extended picture essay on the joys of journeying via Deutsche Bundesbahn.

"Our baggage car has a capacity of 134,670 liters," this ad boasted—ample space, it would seem, for a caravan of trunk-toting passengers.

Unlike automobiles, trains hardly ever need to stop for red lights. Signals are always "grün . . . grün . . . grün" on the Bundesbahn.

Fancy cars are "dreams on wheels," reads the headline. The Bundesbahn's dream vehicle was this 8,430-horsepower super-fast engine.

A Big Splash in Posters

Effective posters, like good newspaper headlines, tell their story at a glance. They rivet people's attention with bold, dramatic design and deliver their message in the briefest possible terms. Traditionally this purpose has been achieved by graphic artists using vivid colors and arresting shapes. But poster designers sometimes turn to photography to provide the impact, as well as the sense of immediacy that illustrations cannot always convey.

"We picked a photograph to show the excitement of modern horse racing," said Gus Boyd, who helped to create this poster for New York's Aqueduct race track. "Photography," he explains, "means now—today." □

To announce the racing season at New York's Aqueduct, McCann-Erickson's Gus Boyd shot his own photograph of action on the track.

Appendix

Equipment for Photojournalists

35mm cameras. *Handy and versatile, these small, lightweight cameras have become the favorites of photojournalists in the years since World War II. They enable photographers not only to get close to the action, but to move swiftly from point to point, obtaining a variety of views as a story unfolds. Minimum interference with the story is another premium of the small size. Scarcely noticeable in the hands of an expert news photographer, the camera does not intrude into the action, making the subjects of the story self-conscious about its presence. Moreover, the 35mm camera can be very rapidly operated—focused, shot and the next frame advanced—within seconds. This fact, coupled with the large number of exposures available on a roll—20 or 36—is of enormous help to the photographer seeking a series of related action shots—whether his story is a ball game, a riot or a political rally. Many press photographers use the rangefinder type of 35mm camera—it is quiet and, under some circumstances, easy to focus—but SLRs like the Nikon F above are now the most popular. Their through-the-lens focusing is valuable, but their big advantage is the ease with which they can be fitted with a variety of lenses from wide-angle to telephoto. Larger SLRs—such as the 2¼ x 2¼ Hasselblad—are also frequently used by photojournalists.*

Twin-lens reflex. *Almost as popular with photojournalists as the SLR, a twin-lens reflex like the Rolleiflex above offers certain advantages over the single-lens; many photographers on assignment carry both. The SLR makes a loud click when its shutter is operated; the twin-lens is virtually silent in operation, an important consideration in covering such an event as a golf match or a symphony. The relatively large viewing screen on top of the twin-lens simplifies fast, precise composition and has some other advantages as well. If the camera is held upside down, it can shoot over the heads of a crowd and, swiveled sideways, it can sneak a candid shot while the photographer seems to aim innocently forward. It is not, however, as handy for candid work as the smaller SLR and, on most models, lenses are not interchangeable. The twin-lens, therefore, is largely used for feature rather than action stories.*

Small modular cameras. *This comparatively new type combines much of the versatility of the standard press camera (described at far right) with lightweight handiness like that of 35mm and 2¼ x 2¼ cameras. Each can be ordered with a wide choice of fittings: ground-glass focusing screen, rangefinder coupled to the lens (as with the Graflex XL shown above), optical or open-wire viewfinders, and a broad range of lenses. Parts are sold individually to make up a modular "camera system." The negative size can be relatively large (a maximum of 2¼ x 3¼) so that enlargement for newspaper work is not essential, or smaller, depending on the kind of film back fitted to the camera.*

Polaroid Land Camera. *Sometimes thought of as an instrument designed purely for amateurs, the Polaroid Land Camera is a cherished professional tool on hundreds of weeklies and small dailies. Its almost foolproof operation enables reporters with little photographic training to get good pictures. The 3¼ x 4¼ pictures are large enough for a harried editor to judge without a magnifying glass, and most important of all, the instantly available prints can be sent directly to the engraver without darkroom processing—an obvious advantage under the pressure of deadlines, aside from being a cost saver. A special film pack, usable on some models, can produce not only positives but negatives to make additional prints for presentation to local celebrities —a good-will practice sometimes followed by small papers.*

Standard press cameras. *The Speed Graphic above is the best-known example of the camera that once dominated photojournalism. It is a portable version of the view camera used for studio photography, and can do almost everything a view camera can: the lens mount is removable, permitting the use of almost any lens and moves up and down and tilts to compensate for optical distortions; the bellows extends to extra length for extreme close-ups. But some press cameras can do more than view cameras, for many models have two independent focusing devices: a view camera's ground-glass screen, for through-the-lens focusing and, in addition, a coupled rangefinder for fast focusing. Also fitted are an open wire-frame and an optical viewfinder. Interchangeable backs are available, so that sheet film, roll film or Polaroid Land film can be used. The standard model makes a picture in the 4 x 5 size, which happens to be very handy for newspaper work. Five inches is the width of three newspaper columns; thus a contact print can be dropped intact into a three-column space without cropping or enlargement. All this versatility, however, must be balanced against the press camera's size, weight and general clumsiness. Such cameras are now used mainly to cover sports events, parades and inaugurations when the photographer is forced to remain in a fixed position.*

A Specialized Tool for Fast Action

A number of cameras can be adapted to make a series of photographs to show a sequence of steps in fast action, such as the take-off of Apollo 11 at right. One that is designed specifically for this purpose is the Hulcher *(below)*. Superficially it resembles a movie camera, exposing one frame at a time as film moves intermittently past the lens. Unlike a movie camera, however, it is virtually vibrationless—assuring sharp pictures—because of an ingenious film-advance mechanism *(diagram, opposite)*. It is also versatile in ways that are important for action stills, taking as few as five or as many as 75 frames a second at shutter speeds from 1/25 second to, in some special models, 1/34,000 second. Hulchers are now coming into widespread use to cover baseball, football and hockey, recording entire sequences of a complete action or simply providing a large selection of action pictures for an editor to choose from.

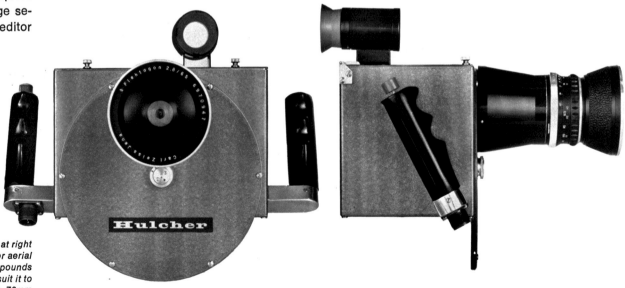

Although the Hulcher 108 model shown at right in front and side views was designed for aerial photography, its light weight (five pounds without lens) and convenient hand grips suit it to fast-action press photography. It uses 70mm film, providing 2¼ x 5 negatives when set to take 25 frames per second or 2¼ x 2½ negatives when shooting 50 frames per second —but it will not be found in every photographer's kitbag. The price of the Hulcher 108 is $1,700.

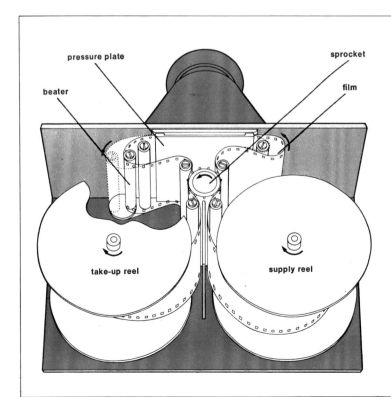

pressure plate

sprocket

film

beater

take-up reel

supply reel

The Hulcher gains steadiness for unblurred action pictures from mechanisms that rotate continuously instead of starting and stopping (as most camera mechanisms do)—yet make the film stop for each exposure as shown at left. Film is led off the supply reel via a continuously turning sprocket, building up into a loop (solid and dotted lines at left). Intermittently it moves from this loop to stop between pressure plate and lens for a picture, being pulled by the "beater" and then fed via the sprocket onto the take-up reel. The key element is the beater, a shaft mounted on the outer edge of a continuously rotating disk. When the eccentrically revolving beater is turned toward the right (solid lines), the film is stationary. At that instant, a spinning disk mounted between the lens and the pressure plate lines up a wedge-shaped slit with the lens—and light can reach the film to take a picture. Then the slit moves away as the beater turns to the left (dotted lines), presses the film surface and once again pulls the film forward.

A Lens to Annihilate Distance

The Astro-Telestan F/10 shown at right mounted on a Nikon Model F is a behemoth among lenses. At 2,000mm its focal length is 40 times longer than that of the normal lens (50mm) for a 35mm camera (for comparison, a normally equipped Nikon is shown at its right). This huge lens provides greatly enlarged images of distant objects (40 times what the human eye sees or a normal lens shows), using a relatively simple optical system. In many long lenses greater focal length is obtained by increasing the distance traveled by entering light rays before they reach the film. The light rays are bounced back and forth between mirrors mounted within the housing. Alternatively, the distance traveled by the entering light rays may be increased simply by extending the physical length of the lens housing. The Telestan is six and one half feet in length.

Like the Hulcher sequence camera, the 2,000mm lens is a highly specialized professional tool that is employed on important assignments when even a relatively long lens, such as a 125 to 400mm, cannot obtain sufficiently large pictures of a distant subject—perhaps an Apollo splashdown in the Pacific, when the shooting platform is an aircraft carrier two miles or more from impact point.

So long a focal length, and the enormous magnification produced, can create special problems. Haze or smog build up so much over long shooting distances that the big lens is really successful only in clear air. The slightest quiver—which is magnified just as much as the image is—results in a blurred picture; special tripods must be used to give the lens rock-firm support.

Both taken from the same spot in a New York building, the pictures above demonstrate the magnifying power of the 2,000mm Telestan. The one at top, made with a 50mm lens, shows nearby buildings and a distant view of the New Jersey skyline. The small boxed area in this picture is the view included in the bottom picture taken with the Telestan, bringing close to the eye buildings nearly three miles distant.

Bibliography

General

De Maré, Eric, *Photography*. Penguin Books, 1968

Gernsheim, Helmut, *Creative Photography: Aesthetic Trends 1839-1960*. Faber and Faber Ltd., 1962.

Gernsheim, Helmut and Alison, *The Recording Eye: A Hundred Years of Great Events as seen by the Camera*. G. P. Putnam's Sons, 1960.

Neblette, Carroll B., *Photography: Its Materials and Processes*. D. Van Nostrand, 1962.

Whiting, John R., *Photography is a Language*. Ziff-Davis, 1946.

History

Baldwin, Sidney, *Poverty and Politics: The Rise and Decline of the Farm Security Administration*. University of North Carolina Press, 1968.

Darrah, William Culp, *Stereo Views: A History of Stereographs in America and Their Collection*. Times and News Publishing, 1964.

*Goldston, Robert, *The Great Depression: The United States in the Thirties*. Bobbs-Merrill, 1968.

McWilliams, Carey, *Ill Fares the Land: Migrants and Migratory Labor in the United States*. Little, Brown, 1942.

Mott, Frank Luther, *American Journalism: A History 1690-1960*. Macmillan, 1969.

Newhall, Beaumont, *The History of Photography from 1839 to the Present Day*. The Museum of Modern Art, Doubleday, 1964.

Phillips, Cabell, *From the Crash to the Blitz*. Macmillan, 1969.

Pollack, Peter, *The Picture History of Photography*. Harry N. Abrams, 1958.

Raper, Arthur F., and Ira De A. Reid, *Sharecroppers All*. University of North Carolina Press, 1941.

*Taft, Robert, *Photography and the American Scene: A Social History 1839-1889*. Dover Publications, 1964.

Biography

Eisenstaedt, Alfred, and Arthur Goldsmith, eds., *The Eye of Eisenstaedt*. Viking, 1969.

Horan, James D., *Mathew Brady: Historian with a Camera*. Crown Publishers, 1955.

Juergens, George, *Joseph Pulitzer and the New York World*. Princeton University Press, 1966.

Special Fields

Faber, John, *Great Moments in News Photography*. Thomas Nelson & Sons, 1960.

Ford, James L. C., *Magazines for Millions*. Southern Illinois University Press, 1969.

Rhode, Robert B., and Floyd H. McCall, *Press Photography: Reporting with a Camera*. Macmillan, 1961.

Rothstein, Arthur, *Photojournalism: Pictures for Magazines and Newspapers*. Chilton, 1965.

*Rothstein, Arthur, John Vachon, and Roy Stryker, *Just Before the War: Urban America from 1935 to 1941 as seen by photographers of the Farm Security Administration*. October House, 1968.

Schuneman, Raymond Smith, *The Photograph in Print: An Examination of New York Daily Newspapers, 1890-1937*. University Microfilms, University of Minnesota, 1966.

†Steichen, Edward, ed., *The Bitter Years: 1935-1941: Rural America as seen by the photographers of the Farm Security Administration*. The Museum of Modern Art, Doubleday, 1962.

Magazines

Camera, C. J. Bucher Ltd., Lucerne, Switzerland

Infinity, American Society of Magazine Photographers, New York City

Journalism Quarterly, Association for Education in Journalism, Iowa City, Iowa

Modern Photography, The Billboard Publishing Co., New York City

Popular Photography, Ziff-Davis Publishing Co. New York City

U.S. Camera, U.S. Camera Publishing Corp., New York City

*Also available in paperback
†Available only in paperback

Acknowledgments

For the help given in the preparation of this book, the editors would like to express their gratitude to the following: Juergen Arnold, Public Relations Manager, German Federal Railroad General Agency for North America, New York City; Peter C. Bunnell, Curator, Department of Photography, The Museum of Modern Art, New York City; Howard Chapnick, Black Star Publishing Co., Inc., New York City; Alma Eshenfelder and Virginia Ewalt, Publicity Department, Marine Historical Association, Mystic, Connecticut; Helen M. Hinkle, New York City; T. T. Holden, Photo Products, The Singer Company, Graflex Division, Rochester, New York; Charles A. Hulcher, President, Charles A. Hulcher Co., Inc., Hampton, Virginia; Peter Hunter, Press Features, Amsterdam, Holland; André Kertèsz, New York City; Kate Bulls LaFayette, Director, KLH Child Development Center, Inc., Cambridge, Massachusetts; Stefan Lorant and John Furbish, Lenox, Massachusetts; Tom Lovcik, Department of Photography, The Museum of Modern Art, New York City; Grace M. Mayer, Curator, Steichen Collection, Department of Photography, The Museum of Modern Art, New York City; Charles Rado, Rapho Guillumette, New York City; Jens Risom, New York City; Ira Sacher, Manager, and George Fry, Manager of Camera Department, Willoughby-Peerless Camera Stores, New York City; Cheryl and Melvin Sparks, New York City; Humphrey Sutton, New York City; John Szarkowski, Director, Department of Photography, The Museum of Modern Art, New York City; Valerie Vondermuhll, Litchfield, Connecticut, and Phyllis Wise, McLean, Virginia.

Picture Credits *Credits from left to right are separated by semicolons, from top to bottom by dashes.*

COVER—Bill Eppridge for LIFE. Printed by Herb Orth.

Chapter 1: 11—United Press International. 13 —*The Illustrated London News,* courtesy New York Public Library. 14—Mathew Brady, courtesy Library of Congress. 15—*Harper's Weekly,* courtesy New York Public Library. 16,17 —Photographs by Alfred Eisenstaedt for LIFE. Drawing by Nicholas Fasciano. 18,19—*Daily News,* courtesy New York Public Library. 20,21 —Army-Navy Task Force photo, courtesy Wide World. 22—John D. Daniels, courtesy Gernsheim Collection, Humanities Research Center, The University of Texas at Austin. 23—NASA for LIFE. 24,25—Al Muto for United Press International; John D. Collins for Wide World. 26,27—© Associated Press of Great Britain, Ltd. 28—Interphoto. 29—Margaret Bourke-White for LIFE—Tom McAvoy for LIFE. 30—Bill Eppridge for LIFE. 31—Yasushi Nagao, courtesy United Press International. 32—Edward Clark for LIFE. 33—© Keystone Press Agency, Ltd. 34,35 —George Silk for LIFE. 36—H. S. ("Newsreel") Wong, courtesy United Press International. 37 —Hector Rondon, courtesy Wide World. 38 —Arnold Genthe, courtesy Museum of Modern Art, New York. 39—Carl Nesensohn for Wide World. 40—William W. Dyviniak, courtesy Wide World. 41—I. Russell Sorgi for *Buffalo Courier-Express.* 42—George Silk for LIFE. 43—Roger Bockrath for *San Rafael Independent-Journal.* 44 —Central Press Photos, Ltd. 45—I. Wilmer Counts for *Arkansas Democrat.* 46—Nat Fein for Wide World. 47—Morris Berman for *Pittsburgh Post Gazette.* 48—Sy Friedman for NBC. 49 —Arthur Fellig ("Weegee"). 50—Lisa Larsen for LIFE.

Chapter 2: 53—Erich Salomon, © Peter Hunter, Press Features, Amsterdam. 56—Courtesy *The Illustrated London News,* Dec. 12, 1915. Copied by Paulus Leeser. 57—Courtesy *The Illustrated London News,* Nov. 16, 1918, and Humphrey Sutton. The photographs on pages 58 through 61, 66 and 67 are from the Collection of Stefan Lorant and are copied by Paulus Leeser. 58 —Felix Man for *Münchner Illustrierte Presse,* 1929, courtesy Suddeutscher Verlag, Munich. 59 —*Münchner Illustrierte Presse,* 1929, courtesy Suddeutscher Verlag, Munich. 60—Felix Man

for *Münchner Illustrierte Presse,* 1930-31. 61 —Brassaï from Rapho Guillumette for *Weekly Illustrated,* Dec. 1, 1934. 63,64,65—Margaret Bourke-White for LIFE. 66,67—Robert Capa from Magnum for *Picture Post,* May 3, 1938. 68 through 71—Leonard McCombe for LIFE. 72 through 81—W. Eugene Smith for LIFE. 82 through 85—Bill Eppridge for LIFE. 87 through 92—© Brian Brake from Rapho Guillumette. Top layout, courtesy LIFE; bottom layout, courtesy *Paris-Match.*

Chapter 3: 95—Courtesy State Historical Society of Wisconsin. 98,99—Sebastian Milito. 100,101 —Yale Joel. 102,103—Marcia Keegan. 104,105 —Michael Semak. 106,107—Robert Walch. 108,109—Tim Kantor. 110,111—William Kuykendall. 112,113—Joel Snyder. 114,115—U.S. Air Force, courtesy Wide World. 116,117—Alfred Eisenstaedt for LIFE. 119 through 134—All photographs were taken for the Farm Security Administration and are from the Collections of the Library of Congress. 119—Russell Lee. 120 —Carl Mydans. 121—Ben Shahn; Dorothea Lange. 122—John Vachon. 123—Dorothea Lange. 124—Walker Evans. 125—Arthur Rothstein. 126 through 133—Dorothea Lange. 134—Marion Post Wolcott.

Chapter 4: 137—Evelyn Hofer. 140 through 145 —Henry Humphrey. 146 through 151—Evelyn Hofer. 152 through 155—Sebastian Milito. 156 through 161—Courtesy Valerie Vondermuhll. 162 —Constantine Manos from Magnum. 163—John Zimmerman for LIFE. 164,165—Edward Steichen, courtesy Museum of Modern Art, New York. Copied by Paulus Leeser. 166, 167, 168—Don Hinkle. Map, page 166, copied by Herb Orth.

Chapter 5: 171—Alfred Eisenstaedt for LIFE. 174 through 190—Leonard McCombe for LIFE.

Chapter 6: 193—John Condon, courtesy Office of Congressman Edward I. Koch. 196—David G. Fitzgerald, courtesy American Greetings Corp. An American Greetings Soft Touch Card; Jack Zehrt from FPG, courtesy Empathy Graphics, Inc. 197—Courtesy Roberto Benedetti, Rome; Michel Huet, courtesy Editions Hoa-Qui, Paris; Norman Myers, courtesy Sapra Studio, Nairobi —Bruno Bernard, courtesy Arthur F. Krüger

Studio; Centorio Gonzalez Sicilia, courtesy Ediciones Sicilia, Zaragoza. 198—Louis Beringer, courtesy Beringer and Pampaluchi. 199—Leonard Lee Rue III, courtesy National Audubon Society. 200—Suzanne Turner, courtesy Chemical Bank. 201—Stanley E. Sedney; Will Casey; Joel Cagwin; Roy M. Ackerman. All photographs courtesy Aluminum Company of America. 202,203—Harald Sund, courtesy Pacific Northwest Bell. 204—Del Mulkey, reprinted from *Ski Magazine,* Sept. 1970. 205—Michel Proulx and Ted Gorchev, reprinted from *Progressive Architecture,* May 1970. 206—Marilyn Silverstone from Magnum, courtesy Farrar, Straus & Giroux, Inc.; Wide World, courtesy Penguin Books, Inc. 207 —Rowland Scherman, courtesy Simon & Schuster, Inc.; Richard Bluestein, courtesy Cornerstone Library, Inc.; copyright © 1970 by Leon Harris from *The Russian Ballet School,* used by permission of Atheneum Publishers. 208 —Raymond Ross, courtesy Flying Dutchman Productions, Ltd.; William Duevell, © 1968 by ABC Records, Inc. 209—David Gahr, courtesy Vanguard Recording Society, Inc.; Michel Hétier, courtesy Barclay, Compagnie Phonographique Française. 210—Simpson Kalisher, courtesy Wallace-Murray Corporation. 211—Simpson Kalisher, courtesy Bangor Punta Corporation—Bernard Wolf, courtesy Norlin Corporation. 212—Robert Freson, courtesy the Jamaica Tourist Board and Doyle Dane Bernbach, Inc. 213—Wide World, courtesy the International Ladies' Garment Workers' Union and Solow/Wexton, Inc.; Ernst Haas from Magnum, courtesy General Mills, Inc., and Knox Reeves Advertising—Jan Czyrba from Advance Art, courtesy Addressograph Multigraph Corp. and Griswold-Eshleman Co. 214,215—Hans Maier and the McCann-Erickson Archives; Reinhart Wolf; Horst Munzig and Klaus Zimmermann; Hans Maier; Horst Baumann; Reinhart Wolf. All of the photographs on pages 214 and 215 are courtesy the Deutsche Bundesbahn and McCann-Erickson, Inc., Frankfurt, Germany. 216—Gus Boyd, courtesy the New York Racing Association and McCann-Erickson, Inc. 219—Harold Zipkowitz. 220,221 —Ralph Morse for LIFE—Harold Zipkowitz. Drawing by Nicholas Fasciano. 222—Harold Zipkowitz; Walter Daran (2).

Text Credit

Chapter 6: 202,203—Text by e. e. cummings from his poem "since feeling is first," copyright 1926, by Horace Liveright, renewed, 1954, by e. e. cummings. Reprinted by permission of Harcourt Brace Jovanovich, Inc. and MacGibbon and Kee Ltd.

Index
Numerals in italics indicate a photograph, painting or drawing of the subject mentioned.